T0206982

IoT Projects with Arduino Nano 33 BLE Sense

Step-By-Step Projects for Beginners

Agus Kurniawan

Apress®

IoT Projects with Arduino Nano 33 BLE Sense: Step-By-Step Projects for Beginners

Agus Kurniawan
Faculty of Computer Science, Universitas Indonesia, Depok, Indonesia

ISBN-13 (pbk): 978-1-4842-6457-7 ISBN-13 (electronic): 978-1-4842-6458-4
https://doi.org/10.1007/978-1-4842-6458-4

Managing Director, Apress Media LLC: Welmoed Spahr
Acquisitions Editor: Natalie Pao
Development Editor: James Markham
Coordinating Editor: Jessica Vakili

Distributed to the book trade worldwide by Springer Science+Business Media New York, 1 NY Plaza, New York, NY 10014. Phone 1-800-SPRINGER, fax (201) 348-4505, e-mail orders-ny@springer-sbm.com, or visit www.springeronline.com. Apress Media, LLC is a California LLC and the sole member (owner) is Springer Science + Business Media Finance Inc (SSBM Finance Inc). SSBM Finance Inc is a **Delaware** corporation.

For information on translations, please e-mail booktranslations@springernature.com; for reprint, paperback, or audio rights, please e-mail bookpermissions@springernature.com.

Apress titles may be purchased in bulk for academic, corporate, or promotional use. eBook versions and licenses are also available for most titles. For more information, reference our Print and eBook Bulk Sales web page at http://www.apress.com/bulk-sales.

Any source code or other supplementary material referenced by the author in this book is available to readers on GitHub via the book's product page, located at www.apress.com/978-1-4842-6457-7. For more detailed information, please visit http://www.apress.com/source-code.

Printed on acid-free paper

Table of Contents

TABLE OF CONTENTS

About the Author

Agus Kurniawan is a lecturer, IT consultant, and author. He has 20 years of experience in various software and hardware development projects, delivering materials in training and workshops, and technical writing. He has been awarded the Microsoft Most Valuable Professional (MVP) award 16 years in a row.

Agus is a lecturer and researcher in the field of networking and security systems at the Faculty of Computer Science, Universitas Indonesia, Indonesia. Currently, he is pursuing a PhD in computer science at the Freie Universität Berlin, Germany. He can be reached on Twitter at @agusk2010.

About the Technical Reviewer

Sai Yamanoor is an embedded systems engineer working for an industrial gases company in Buffalo, New York. His interests, deeply rooted in DIY and open source hardware, include developing gadgets that aid behavior modification. He has published two books with his brother and in his spare time, he likes to contribute to building things that improve quality of life. You can find his project portfolio at `http://saiyamanoor.com`.

CHAPTER 1

Setting up a Development Environment

Arduino Nano 33 BLE Sense is an Internet of Things (IoT) solution to perform sensing and actuating on a physical environment. The Arduino Nano 33 BLE Sense board comes with a Bluetooth low energy (BLE) module and some built-in sensors that enable us to build an IoT application-based BLE network. This chapter explores how to set up the Arduino Nano 33 BLE Sense board for development.

The following topics are covered in this chapter:

- Reviewing the Arduino Nano 33 BLE Sense board

- Setting up a development environment

- Building a blinking LED program

- Using Arduino web editor

© Agus Kurniawan 2021
A. Kurniawan, *IoT Projects with Arduino Nano 33 BLE Sense*,
https://doi.org/10.1007/978-1-4842-6458-4_1

Introduction

Arduino Nano 33 BLE Sense is one of the IoT platforms from Arduino. This board uses an nRF52840 module with some built-in sensors. The nRF52840 module provides the BLE network stack that is used to communicate with other devices. Bluetooth is a component of a wireless personal area network (WPAN) that enables a devices to communicate with other devices within a short distance.

The Arduino Nano 33 BLE Sense board is designed for low-cost IoT devices to address your IoT problems. At 45 × 18 mm (length × width), the Arduino Nano 33 BLE Sense is compact, as you can see in Figure 1-1.

Figure 1-1. *Arduino Nano 33 BLE Sense board*

Reviewing the Arduino Nano 33 BLE Sense Board

Arduino Nano 33 BLE Sense is built from nRF52840. The board also has a radio-module-based BLE. This module is designed for data communication over Bluetooth. The detailed specifications of Arduino Nano 33 BLE Sense are shown in Table 1-1.

Table 1-1. *Specifications of Arduino Nano 33 BLE Sense*

Feature	Notes
Microcontroller	nRF52840
Secure module	ATECC608A
Operating voltage	3.3V
Input voltage	21V
DC current per I/O pin (limit)	15 mA
Clock speed	64 Mhz
CPU flash memory	1 MB (bRF52840)
SRAM	256 KB
EEPROM	None
Digital I/O	14
PWM pins	All digital pins
UART	1
SPI	1
I2C	1
Analog input	8 (ADC 12-bit 200k sample)

(*continued*)

3

Table 1-1. *(continued)*

Feature	Notes
Analog output	Only through PWM (no DAC)
LED_BUILTIN	13
USB	Native in the nRF52840 processor
IMU	LSM9DSI
Microphone	MP34DT05
Gesture, light, proximity	APDS9960
Barometric pressure	LPS22HB
Temperature, humidity	HTS221
Size (length × width)	45 mm × 18 mm

Because Arduino Nano 33 BLE Sense has some digital and analog input/output (I/O), we extend the board's capabilities by wiring with other sensors or actuators. We also use UART, Serial Peripheral Interface (SPI), and I2C protocols to communicate with other devices.

You can see in Table 1-1 that Arduino Nano 33 BLE Sense has some internal sensor devices that you can use for your IoT solutions. We explore these sensor devices further in Chapter 3.

Next, we set up Arduino Nano 33 BLE Sense on your computer so you can build programs for the Arduino board.

Setting up a Development Environment

Arduino provides software to build programs for all Arduino board models. This software is available for Windows, Linux, and macOS, and it can be downloaded from https://www.arduino.cc/en/Main/Software.

The installation process is easy, following the installation guidelines from Arduino setup. After installation is complete, you will see the Arduino application menu on the main menu in your OS platform.

When you open the Arduino application, you will see the application screen shown in Figure 1-2. Skeleton code is included in the application dialog box. The following is a code template.

```
void setup() {
  // put your setup code here, to run once:
}

void loop() {
  // put your main code here, to run repeatedly:
}
```

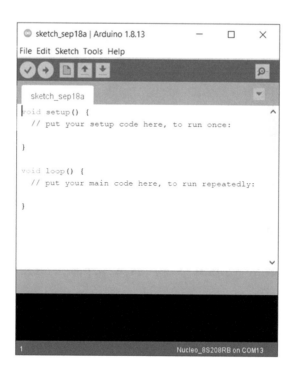

Figure 1-2. *Arduino software for Windows*

The Arduino program adopts C/C++ program language dialects. We can put all data initialization in the setup() function. The program will execute codes inside the loop() function continuously.

To work with the Arduino Nano 33 BLE Sense board, we need to configure the Arduino software. First, add Arduino nRF528x Boards so Arduino software will recognize the Arduino Nano 33 BLE Sense board. On the Arduino menu bar, click Tools ➤ Board ➤ Boards Manager. That will open the Boards Manager dialog box shown in Figure 1-3. In the Type drop-down list, select All. Type Arduino&Nano&33&BLE in the accompanying text box. You will see Arduino nRF528x Boards listed. Click Install to install this package, after you have checked that your computer is connected to the Internet.

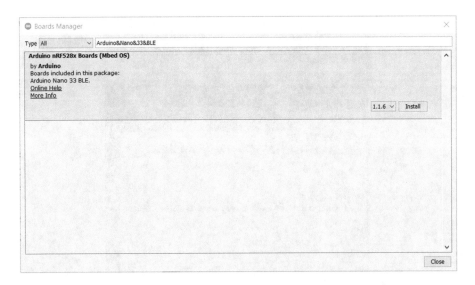

Figure 1-3. *Adding supported boards for Arduino Nano 33 BLE Sense*

This installation takes several minutes to complete. Once it is installed, you can see the Arduino Nano 33 BLE Sense board on the targeted board. You can verify it by selecting Tools ➤ Board ➤ Boards Manager in the Arduino software to view your board list. Figure 1-4 shows the Arduino Nano 33 BLE Sense board in the Arduino software.

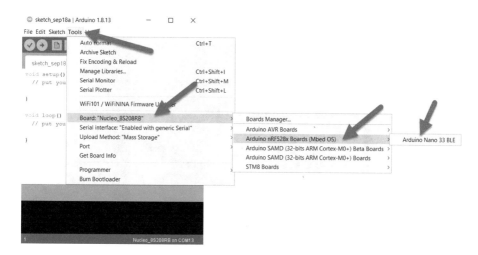

Figure 1-4. *A list of targeted boards for Arduino*

Next, attach the Arduino Nano 33 BLE Sense board to the computer via a micro USB cable. After it is attached, you can verify your board using Device Manager for Windows. Figure 1-5 shows my Arduino Nano 33 BLE Sense on Windows 10.

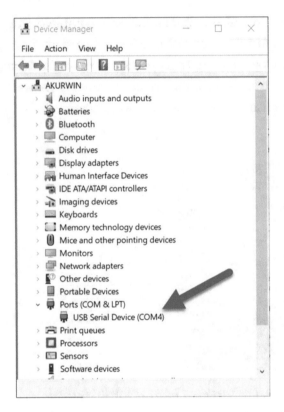

Figure 1-5. *Detected Arduino Nano 33 BLE Sense board on Device Manager in Windows 10*

If you are working on Linux, you can verify Arduino Nano 33 BLE Sense using this terminal command:

```
$ ls /dev/ttyUSB*
```

You will see a list of attached devices over USB. Arduino Nano 33 BLE Sense usually is detected as /dev/ttyUSB0 or /dev/ttyUSB1. For macOS, you can type this command to check for Arduino Nano 33 BLE Sense:

```
$ ls /dev/cu*
```

You should see a USB device on your terminal.

Hello Arduino: Blinking LED

Now that you have connected Arduino Nano 33 BLE Sense to a computer, you can start to write Arduino programs. The Arduino Nano 33 BLE Sense board has a built-in LED that is attached on digital pin 13. In this section, we build a simple blinking LED.

First, open the Arduino software and create a program from project template. Click File ➤ Examples ➤ 01.Basics ➤ Blink. This will display the sample program codes shown in Figure 1-6.

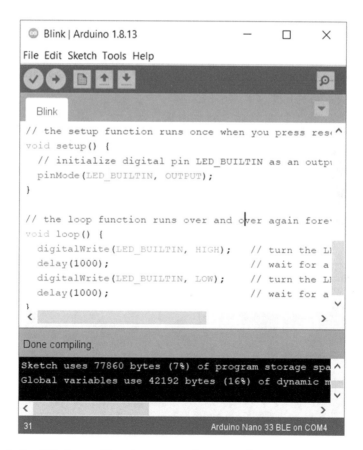

Figure 1-6. *Blink application on Arduino software*

The program code is written as follows.

```
void setup() {
  // initialize digital pin LED_BUILTIN as an output.
  pinMode(LED_BUILTIN, OUTPUT);
}

// the loop function runs over and over again forever
void loop() {
  digitalWrite(LED_BUILTIN, HIGH);    // turn the LED on (HIGH
                                      is the voltage level)
  delay(1000);                        // wait for a second
  digitalWrite(LED_BUILTIN, LOW);     // turn the LED off by
                                      making the voltage LOW
  delay(1000);                        // wait for a second
}
```

Save this program. The next step is to compile and upload the Arduino program into Arduino Nano 33 BLE Sense. Click the Verify icon to compile the Arduino program. To upload the Arduino program into the board, the click Upload icon. Both of these icons are highlighted in Figure 1-7.

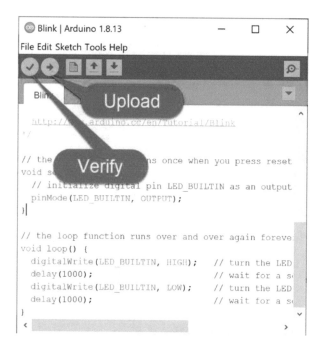

Figure 1-7. *Compiling and flashing a program*

Before you upload a program, you can select Arduino Nano 33 BLE Sense. Select Tools ➤ Board ➤ Arduino nRF528x Boards (Mbed OS) ➤ Arduino Nano 33 BLE, as shown in Figure 1-8. You also need to select the Arduino port. To do so, select Tools ➤ Port and then select your COM port. For instance, my Arduino Nano 33 BLE Sense port is COM4, as shown in Figure 1-9.

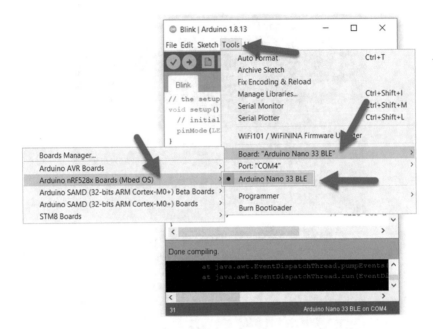

Figure 1-8. *Selecting the Arduino Nano 33 BLE Sense board*

Figure 1-9. *Selecting the port for an Arduino board*

After uploading this Arduino program into Arduino Nano 33 BLE Sense, we will see a blinking LED on the Arduino Nano 33 BLE Sense board, as shown in Figure 1-10.

Figure 1-10. *Blinking LED on Arduino Nano 33 BLE Sense board*

How does this work? The Arduino Nano 33 BLE Sense board has one built-in LED on digital pin 13. In our program, we set digital pin 13 as the digital output using pinMode(). We initialize this data on the setup() function.

```
void setup() {
  // initialize digital pin LED_BUILTIN as an output.
  pinMode(LED_BUILTIN, OUTPUT);
}
```

The Arduino program defines LED_BUILTIN for a general built-in LED pin. We can set the pin as the output mode by giving a value, OUTPUT.

Now our program will run continuously with the loop() function, turning on LED and then turning off the LED. We can use digitalWrite() to perform switch the LED on and off. Set the value to HIGH for turning on the LED. Otherwise, we can turn off the LED by sending the value LOW to the digitalWrite() function. We also set a delay of 1000 ms with the delay() function.

```
void loop() {
  digitalWrite(LED_BUILTIN, HIGH);   // turn the LED on (HIGH
                                     //   is the voltage level)
  delay(1000);                       // wait for a second
  digitalWrite(LED_BUILTIN, LOW);    // turn the LED off by
                                     //   making the voltage LOW
  delay(1000);                       // wait for a second
}
```

You can practice experimenting with these settings for the blinking LED program.

Using Arduino Web Editor

Arduino provides an online editor to build Arduino programs. The advantage of this online editor is that you don't need to prepare too many runtimes and tools. You need only a browser and an Internet connection.

You can access the Arduino web editor using any browser by navigating to https://create.arduino.cc/editor. Figure 1-11 shows the Arduino web editor model. To use the Arduino web editor, we must register with the Arduino portal to build Arduino programs.

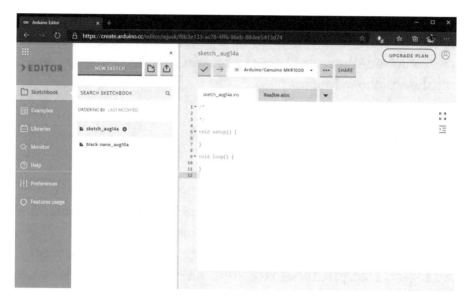

Figure 1-11. *Arduino web editor*

In this section, we focus on getting started with the Arduino web editor by preparing a browser and Internet access. We will perform these tasks to complete our Arduino development with the online web editor:

- Register an Arduino portal account.

- Install the Arduino plug-in.

- Build a blink application for Arduino Nano 33 BLE Sense.

Registering an Arduino Account

To use and build Arduino programs with the Arduino web editor, we must register an Arduino account. This account is similar to the account that is used to buy an Arduino board on the Arduino store.

You can start registering a new Arduino account by clicking the right-top menu icon. You can then fill in the pertinent information to this portal. After completing the account registration, we can build Arduino programs with the Arduino web editor.

Installing the Arduino Plug-in

To enable our Arduino Nano 33 BLE Sense to connect to the Arduino web editor, we need to install the Arduino plug-in. This is required task for Windows. The Arduino plug-in will act as a bridge between the local Arduino Nano 33 BLE Sense board and the Arduino web editor.

First, open a browser and navigate to `https://create.arduino.cc/ getting-started/plugin/welcome`. That will result in the screen shown in Figure 1-12.

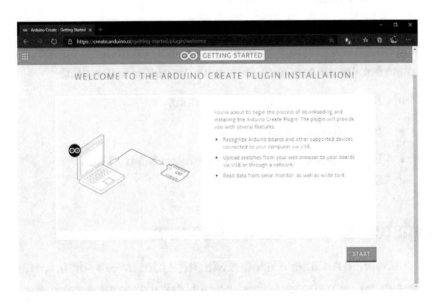

Figure 1-12. *Arduino plug-in installation*

Click Start. You will then see as the screen shown in Figure 1-13. Click Download button to the download Arduino plug-in application.

Figure 1-13. *Downloading the Arduino plug-in for Windows*

After downloading the Arduino plug-in, you can install this application. Follow the installation steps from the setup file. If the Arduino plug-in installation is completed properly, the browser will detect the Arduino plug-in.

Your web editor probably does not detect your Arduino Nano 33 BLE Sense at this point. You can ignore this and continue to build Arduino programs using the Arduino web editor. Next, we build a blink Arduino application.

Building an Arduino Program

The Arduino web editor has the same functionalities as thedesktop version of the Arduino software. The Arduino web editor has project samples, and we can also add Arduino libraries into the project.

In this section, we build a blink Arduino application like the previous project. Start by opening a browser and navigating to `https://create.arduino.cc/editor`. Select Examples from the left menu, then click the BUILTIN tab, and under 01.BASICS(6), select Blink. This is illustrated in Figure 1-14.

After we select the Blink project sample, we have the blink program shown in Figure 1-15. Now we can compile and upload the program into Arduino Nano 33 BLE Sense.

Select your Arduino Nano 33 BLE Sense board on the device drop-down list. Click the Verify icon and then the Upload icon to the left of the drop-down list. This will compile and upload the Arduino program to the targeted board.

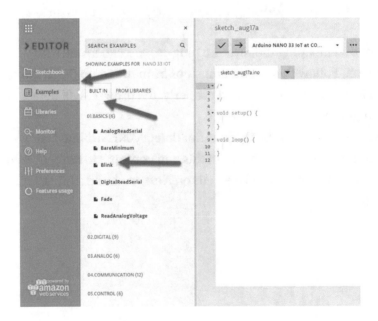

Figure 1-14. *Creating a new project*

Figure 1-15. _Uploading a program into Arduino Nano 33 BLE Sense_

You can try to build another Arduino project using the Arduino web editor with project samples from this tool.

Summary

You have learned to set up an Arduino development environment. You also installed Arduino software on the desktop environment and built a simple Arduino program, blink. In addition, you looked at using the Arduino web editor to build Arduino programs.

Next, you will learn how to access Arduino Nano 33 BLE Sense I/O. We use other communication protocols as well.

CHAPTER 2

Arduino Nano 33 BLE Sense Board Development

This chapter focuses on how to build Arduino Nano 33 BLE Sense programs using Arduino Sketch. This software is available for Windows, macOS, and Linux. We also explore how to access I/O peripherals on Arduino Nano 33 BLE Sense board with Arduino programs.

In this chapter, you will learn about the following topics:

- How to write Arduino programs using Sketch.

- How to access digital I/O.

- How to access analog I/O.

- How to plot analog sensor analog.

- How to build serial communication.

- How to access pulse-width modulation (PWM).

- How to access Serial Peripheral Interface (SPI).

- How to scan I2C an address.

- How to read sensor devices-based I2C.

© Agus Kurniawan 2021
A. Kurniawan, *IoT Projects with Arduino Nano 33 BLE Sense*,
https://doi.org/10.1007/978-1-4842-6458-4_2

Introduction

We can say Arduino is a platform because Arduino as company provides hardware and software. To build programs for Arduino Nano 33 BLE Sense boards, we can use Arduino Sketch. This program uses C/C++ language dialects.

This chapter covers how to build programs for Arduino Nano 33 BLE Sense. The Arduino Nano 33 BLE Sense board uses a Bluetooth module to connect to a network. Bluetooth is a part a WPAN that enables devices to communicate with other devices within a short distance.

We use Arduino software to build Arduino programs. This tool uses the Sketch program, which uses C++ dialects. Let's turn our attention to Sketch programming.

Basic Sketch Programming

In this section, we learn about the Sketch programming language. Technically, Sketch uses C++ dialects, so if you have experience using C++, you can skip this section.

Main Program

The Arduino program has a main program to perform tasks continuously. When we create a program using Arduino software, we have skeleton codes with two functions, setup() and loop(). The complete codes are shown here.

```
void setup() {
  // put your setup code here, to run once:

}
```

```
void loop() {
  // put your main code here, to run repeatedly:

}
```

In this code you can see two functions, setup() and loop(). The setup() function is called once when the Arduino board is to be turned on. If we put codes in the setup() function, it means our codes will run once. Otherwise, we have the loop() function, which is called continuously.

This is a basic structure of the main program from Arduino. In this section, you learn about Sketch programming with the following topics.

- Declaring variables.

- Making conditional statements.

- Making looping.

- Working with break and continue.

Declaring Variables

We can declare a variable using the following statement.

```
<data type> <variable name>;
```

<data type> is a keyword that Sketch adopts from C++. <data type> represents how to define our data type on a variable. <variable name> is the variable name we will call and use in our program. Table 2-1 provides a list of <data type> values used in Sketch.

Table 2-1. *Data Types in Sketch*

array	float	Void
Bool	int	String()
Boolean	long	unsigned char
Byte	short	unsigned int
Char	size_t	unsigned long
Double	string	word

Because the Sketch program adopts from C++, we put ; at the end of the code line. Otherwise, we will get an error while compiling codes. For instance, we declare variables with int and char data types as follows.

```
int a;
int b = 10;
char c;
char d = 'A';
```

We can set an initial value while declaring a variable. For instance, we set int b = 10.

For this demonstration, we create a project for Arduino Nano 33 BLE Sense. First, open the Arduino software and write these codes.

```
void setup() {
  int a = 10;
  int b = 5;

  // initialize serial communication
  Serial.begin(115200);
  while (!Serial) {
    ;
  }

  int c = a + b;
  int d = a * b;
```

```
  // print
  Serial.print("C= ");
  Serial.println(c);

  Serial.print("d= ");
  Serial.println(d);
}
void loop() {
}
```

Figure 2-1 shows this code. To print messages, use the `Serial.print()` and `Serial.println()` functions. We can print messages using `Serial.print()` without a carriage return (`"\r\n"`). Otherwise, we can print messages with a carriage return using `Serial.println()`.

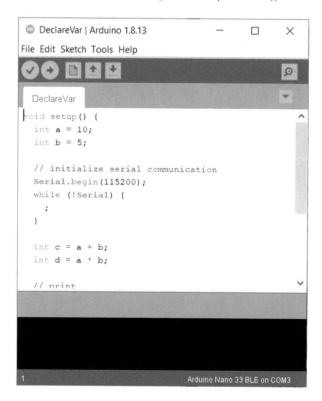

Figure 2-1. *Declaring variables*

All printed messages with the Serial library will be shown on the serial communication channel. Next, save this program, then compile and upload it to the Arduino Nano 33 BLE Sense board.

To see the program output on the serial communication channel, use the Serial Monitor tool from Arduino. To access it, select Tools ➤ Serial Monitor, as shown in Figure 2-2.

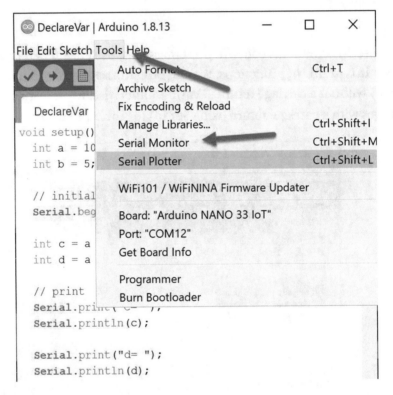

Figure 2-2. *Opening the Serial Monitor tool*

After launching Serial Monitor, you can see your program output, as shown in Figure 2-3. Select a baudrate of 115200 at the bottom of the Serial Monitor console.

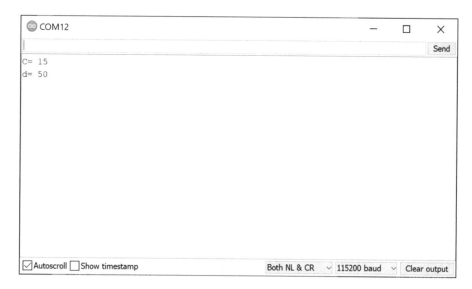

Figure 2-3. *Program output on Serial Monitor*

If you don't see the output message in the Serial Monitor console, you can press the Reset button on the Arduino Nano 33 BLE Sense board. You can find this button next to the micro USB connector, as shown in Figure 2-4.

Figure 2-4. *Position of the Reset button on the Arduino Nano 33 BLE Sense board*

How does this work? This program only runs with the setup() function. We declare two variables, a and b. Then, we assign their values.

```
void setup() {
  int a = 10;
  int b = 5;
```

Next, activate the Serial object to perform serial communication. Set the baud rate to 115200. Use while for looping to wait for the Serial object to be created successfully.

```
// initialize serial communication
  Serial.begin(115200);
  while (!Serial) {
    ;
  }
```

We perform simple mathematical operations such as addition and multiplication. The result of operations is stored in the c and d variables.

```
  int c = a + b;
  int d = a * b;
```

Print the result to the serial terminal using the Serial object.

```
// print
  Serial.print("C= ");
  Serial.println(c);

  Serial.print("d= ");
  Serial.println(d);
```

For the loop() function, do nothing. All code runs on the setup() function. That's why you probably don't see program output; we will see it later.

```
void loop() {
}
```

Operators

Sketch uses C++ operators. Arithmetic operators are declared to perform mathematical operations. We can use the following arithmetic operators:

- % (remainder)
- * (multiplication)
- + (addition)
- - (subtraction)
- / (division)
- = (assignment operator)

For Boolean operators, we implement && for logical and, || for logical or, and ! for logical not.

Conditional Statement

We can perform action-based conditionals. For instance, you might want to turn on a lamp if a light sensor obtains a low intensity value. In Sketch, you can implement conditional statements using if and switch syntax. A conditional statement with if can be declared as follows.

```
if(<conditional>) {
// do something
} else {
// do something
}
```

We can put conditional values in <conditional>, such as applying Boolean and arithmetic operators. For this demo, we can create a Sketch program on Arduino Nano 33 BLE Sense. You can write this complete program.

```
long num_a;
long num_b;
void setup() {
    // initialize serial communication
    Serial.begin(115200);
    while (!Serial) {
        ;
    }
}
void loop() {
    num_a = random(100);
    num_b = random(100);

    // print
    Serial.print("num_a: ");
    Serial.print(num_a);
    Serial.print(", num_b: ");
    Serial.println(num_b);

    if(num_a > num_b) {
        Serial.println("num_a > num_b");
    }else {
        Serial.println("num_a <= num_b");
    }

    delay(2000);
}
```

Save this program as Conditional. Now you can compile and upload this program into the Arduino Nano 33 BLE Sense board. Open Serial Monitor to view the program output, shown in Figure 2-5.

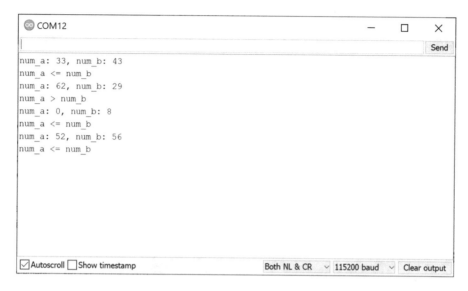

Figure 2-5. Program output for conditional if program

How does this work? This program generates random values for num_a and num_b variables in the loop() function.

```
void loop() {
  num_a = random(100);
  num_b = random(100);
```

Next, print these random values on the serial terminal using the Serial object. We can call the Serial.print() and Serial.println() functions.

```
// print
Serial.print("num_a: ");
Serial.print(num_a);
Serial.print(", num_b: ");
Serial.println(num_b);
```

Finally, we evaluate a value on num_a and num_b using a conditional-if statement. We check if the num_a value is greater than num_b or not. Then, we print the result on the serial terminal.

```
if(num_a > num_b) {
    Serial.println("num_a > num_b");
}else {
  Serial.println("num_a <= num_b");
}
```

The next demonstration is to implement a conditional with a switch statement. In general, we can declare a switch statement as follows.

```
switch(value) {
      case val1: <code>
                break;
      case val2: <code>
                break;
      case val3: <code>
                break;
}
```

For this example, build a program to evaluate the num_a value with a switch statement. Set a random value with a maximum of 5. Open the Arduino software and write this complete program.

```
long num_a;

void setup() {
   // initialize serial communication
  Serial.begin(115200);
  while (!Serial) {
    ;
  }
}
```

```
void loop() {
  num_a = random(5);

  // print
  Serial.print("num_a: ");
  Serial.println(num_a);
  switch(num_a) {
    case 0:
            Serial.println("num_a value is 0");
            break;
    case 1:
            Serial.println("num_a value is 1");
            break;
    case 2:
            Serial.println("num_a value is 2");
            break;
    case 3:
            Serial.println("num_a value is 3");
            break;
    case 4:
            Serial.println("num_a value is 4");
            break;
  }
  delay(2000);
}
```

Save this program as ConditionalSwitch. You can compile and upload this program into the Arduino Nano 33 BLE Sense board. To see the program output, you can open Serial Monitor, as displayed in Figure 2-6.

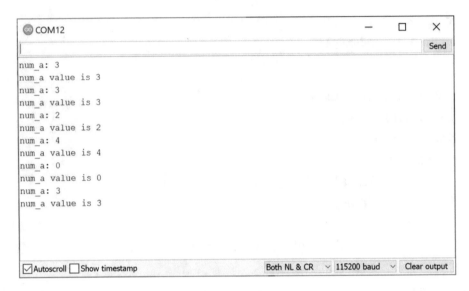

Figure 2-6. Program output for Switch program

How does this work? This program starts to generate random values in the loop() function. The result is stored in the num_a variable. Then, you can print this value to the serial terminal.

```
void loop() {
  num_a = random(5);

  // print
  Serial.print("num_a: ");
  Serial.println(num_a);
```

Next, evaluate the num_a variable using a switch statement. We check num_a for values 0, 1, 2, 3, and 4. We print the message on each switch-case statement.

```
switch(num_a) {
    case 0:
            Serial.println("num_a value is 0");
            break;
```

```
case 1:
        Serial.println("num_a value is 1");
        break;
case 2:
        Serial.println("num_a value is 2");
        break;
case 3:
        Serial.println("num_a value is 3");
        break;
case 4:
        Serial.println("num_a value is 4");
        break;
}
```

You have now learned conditional statements with if and switch. You can use a switch statement if the number of options id fewer than five; otherwise, you can use an if statement with operators.

Looping

A looping task is useful when you perform the same task continuously. In Sketch, you can implement looping tasks using for, while, and do..while statements. Declare a for statement as follows.

```
for(start;conditional;increment/decrement) {
        <codes>
}
```

For a while statement, you can implement it as follows.

```
while(selection) {
        <codes>
}
```

You also can use do..while for looping. You can run the first code step, then select on the while statement.

```
do {
      <codes>
} while(selection);
```

Now you can build a Sketch program to implement looping using for, while, and do..while statements. Write this complete program using the Arduino software.

```
void setup() {
  // initialize serial communication
  Serial.begin(115200);
  while (!Serial) {
    ;
  }
}

void loop() {
  long val = random(15);
  int i;

  // print
  Serial.print("val: ");
  Serial.println(val);

  // looping
  Serial.println("Looping: for");
  for(i=0;i<val;i++){
    Serial.print(i);
    Serial.print(" ");
  }
  Serial.println();
```

```
Serial.println("Looping: while");
int start = 0;
while(start < val) {
  Serial.print(start);
  Serial.print(" ");

  start++;
}
Serial.println();

Serial.println("Looping: do..while");
start = 0;
do {
  Serial.print(start);
  Serial.print(" ");

  start++;
}while(start < val);
Serial.println();

delay(3000);
}
```

You can save this program as Looping, then compile and upload it into the Arduino Nano 33 BLE Sense board. You can then open Serial Monitor to see the program output, as shown in Figure 2-7.

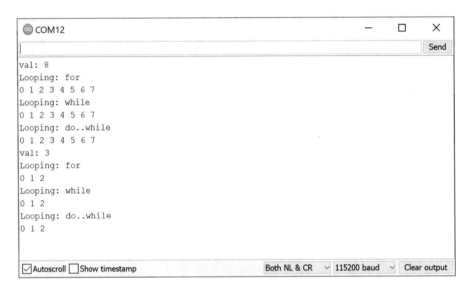

Figure 2-7. *Program output for looping*

How does this work? Set a random value for your looping program.

```
void loop() {
  long val = random(15);
  int i;
```

Next, print this random value to the serial terminal.

```
// print
Serial.print("val: ");
Serial.println(val);
```

For looping with a for statement, perform a loop starting with i=0 until val value.

```
Serial.println("Looping: for");
for(i=0;i<val;i++){
  Serial.print(i);
  Serial.print(" ");
}
Serial.println();
```

For the while statement, perform a similar task to the one for a for statement. Set start = 0 for initialization.

```
int start = 0;
while(start < val) {
  Serial.print(start);
  Serial.print(" ");

  start++;
}
Serial.println();
```

Finally, implement the do..while statement. Set start=0 again, and then perform the looping task.

```
start = 0;
  do {
    Serial.print(start);
    Serial.print(" ");

    start++;
  }while(start < val);
  Serial.println();
```

Break and Continue

When you perform looping, you will likely want to exit the loop or skip a certain step from the loop. In Sketch, you can use break and continue statements.

For this example, we create a Sketch program to perform looping from 0 to a random value. When the looping iteration reaches 5, we skip this step using a continue statement. Then, we exit the loop when we reach an iteration value more than 10 using a break statement.

First, open the Arduino software. Write this complete program for break and continue implementation.

```
void setup() {
  // initialize serial communication
  Serial.begin(115200);
  while (!Serial) {
    ;
  }
}

void loop() {
  long val = random(6, 15);
  int i;

  // print
  Serial.print("val: ");
  Serial.println(val);

  // looping
  Serial.println("Looping: for");
  for(i=0;i<val;i++){
    if(i==5)
      continue;

    if(i>10)
      break;

    Serial.print(i);
    Serial.print(" ");
  }
  Serial.println();

  delay(3000);
}
```

Save this program as BreakContinue, then compile and upload this program into the Arduino Nano 33 BLE Sense board. After uploading the program, you can view the program output using Serial Monitor, as shown in Figure 2-8.

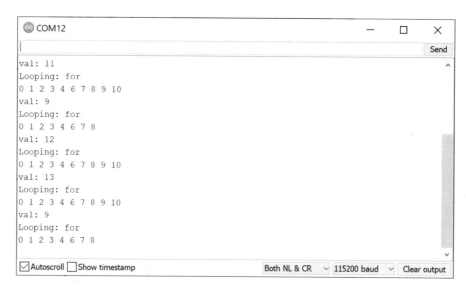

Figure 2-8. *Applying break and continue in Sketch*

How does this work? Set a random value in the loop() function. Print this random value to the serial terminal using the Serial object.

```
void loop() {
  long val = random(6, 15);
  int i;

  // print
  Serial.print("val: ");
  Serial.println(val);
```

Perform looping from 0 to a random value, val. When you have an iteration = 5, skip this iteration using a continue statement. Then, when you have an iteration > 10, exit from looping by calling the break statement.

```
// looping
  Serial.println("Looping: for");
  for(i=0;i<val;i++){
    if(i==5)
      continue;

    if(i>10)
      break;

    Serial.print(i);
    Serial.print(" ");
  }
  Serial.println();
```

This is the end of our basic Sketch program. Next, we write an Arduino program with various cases.

Digital I/O

Arduino Nano 33 BLE Sense has digital input/output on 14 pins. You can attach sensors and actuators in digital I/O pins. The Arduino Nano 33 BLE Sense pin layout is displayed on the back of the board, as shown in Figure 2-9. Digital I/O pins are defined as Dx where x is a digital number; for instance, D1 is digital I/O on pin 1.

Figure 2-9. *Arduino Nano 33 BLE Sense board pinout*

You can check the details of the pinout of the Arduino Nano 33 BLE Sense board on the official Arduino website at https://content.arduino. cc/assets/Pinout-NANOsense_latest.pdf.

To implement a demo for digital I/O on Arduino Nano 33 BLE Sense, we need a LED and a push button. For this examples, use the internal LED (built-in LED) on digital pin 13. We also need a push button that is connected to digital pin 7. Figure 2-10 shows the wiring for this project.

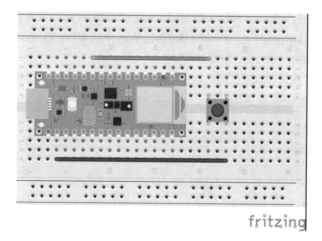

Figure 2-10. *A wiring configuration for a push button project*

Now you can create the Arduino program. This program will turn on an LED when the user presses a push button. The program algorithm is to read a push button state using the digitalRead() function. To turn on the LED, we can use digitalWrite() and set a HIGH value.

Open the Arduino softwareand write this complete program.

```
int led = 13;
int pushButton = 7;
int state = 0;

void setup() {
  pinMode(led, OUTPUT);
  pinMode(pushButton, INPUT);
}
void loop() {
  state = digitalRead(pushButton);
  digitalWrite(led,state);
  delay(300);
}
```

Save this program as ButtonLed, then compile and upload this program to the Arduino Nano 33 BLE Sense board. Once it is uploaded, you can test it by pressing a push button. You should see LED light up on the Arduino Nano 33 BLE Sense.

How does this work? This program starts by initializing values for the LED and push button pins.

```
int led = 13;
int pushButton = 7;
int state = 0;

void setup() {
  pinMode(led, OUTPUT);
  pinMode(pushButton, INPUT);
}
```

Then, in the loop() function, we read a push button state using the digitalRead() function. The state value will be passed to the digitalWrite() function to turn the LED on and off.

```
void loop() {
  state = digitalRead(pushButton);
  digitalWrite(led,state);
  delay(300);
}
```

Now that you've learned about digital I/O, next we look at analog I/O.

Analog I/O

Arduino Nano 33 BLE Sense provides analog I/O to enable us to create interactions with sensor and actuator devices. Analog I/O pins are labeled Ax where x is the analog pin number. You can see these labels on the back of the Arduino Nano 33 BLE Sense board as shown previously in Figure 2-9.

Arduino Nano 33 BLE Sense has eight analog inputs (ADC). Unfortunately, Arduino Nano 33 BLE Sense does not support analog output (DAC), but we can use PWM as analog output. For ADC modeling, Arduino Nano 33 BLE Sense provides ADC resolution with 12 bits.

This demonstration uses an analog temperature sensor, TMP36. You can also use the TMP36 module like a thermal module from Linksprite (see https://www.linksprite.com/wiki/index.php?title=Thermal_ Module). You can perform the wiring shown in Figure 2-11 as follows:

- TMP36 module VCC is connected to Arduino 3.3.V.

- TMP36 module GND is connected to Arduino GND.

- TMP36 module SIG is connected to Arduino analog A0.

Figure 2-11. *Wiring for analog sensor and Arduino Nano 33 BLE Sense*

Now you can write an Arduino program to the analog sensor from the TMP36 module. It will read sensor data and then show it on the serial terminal. Begin by opening the Arduino software and writing this complete program.

```
void setup() {
  Serial.begin(115200);
  while (!Serial) {
    ;
  }
}
```

```
void loop() {
  int reading = analogRead(A0);

  float voltage = reading * 3.3;
  voltage /= 1024.0;

  Serial.print(voltage); Serial.println(" volts");

  float tempC = (voltage - 0.5) * 100 ;

  Serial.print(tempC);
  Serial.println(" degrees C");
  delay(3000);
}
```

Save this program as AnalogSensor. Next, compile and upload this program into the Arduino Nano 33 BLE Sense. Open Serial Monitor to view the program output, which is shown in Figure 2-12.

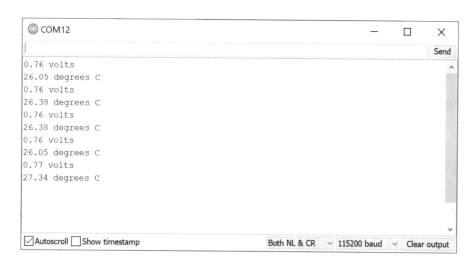

Figure 2-12. *Program output for reading temperature*

How does this work? First, read the sensor data on analog pin A0.

```
void loop() {
  int reading = analogRead(A0);
```

Next, calculate a voltage and show it on the serial terminal. Because we are using a voltage reference of 3.3V, we can calculate using this formula.

```
float voltage = reading * 3.3;
voltage /= 1024.0;

Serial.print(voltage); Serial.println(" volts");
```

Next, compute a temperature using the following formula-based datasheet from the TMP36 module.

```
float tempC = (voltage - 0.5) * 100 ;

Serial.print(tempC);
Serial.println(" degrees C");
```

The result is be printed to the serial terminal.

Plotting an Analog Sensor

You also can plot analog input on a plotter tool that is available in the Arduino software. This example uses a SparkFun Electret Microphone Breakout as the analog source. You can find this module at https://www.sparkfun.com/products/12758.

Connect the SparkFun Electret Microphone Breakout to Arduino Nano 33 BLE Sense board using the following wiring. The resulting configuration is shown in Figure 2-13.

- SparkFun Electret Microphone Breakout module VCC is connected to Arduino 3.3.V.

- SparkFun Electret Microphone Breakout module GND is connected to Arduino GND.

- SparkFun Electret Microphone Breakout module SIG is connected to Arduino A0.

Figure 2-13. *Arduino wiring with SparkFun Electret Microphone Breakout*

Next, you can write an Arduino program to plot sensor data. Open the Arduino software and write this complete program.

```
void setup() {
  Serial.begin(115200);
  while (!Serial) {
    ;
  }
}
```

```
void loop() {
  int val = analogRead(A0);
  Serial.println(val);
  delay(300);
}
```

Save this program as AnalogPlotting, then compile and upload this program into the Arduino Nano 33 BLE Sense. To open the Serial Plotter tool in the Arduino software, on the Tools menu, select Serial Plotter, as shown in Figure 2-14.

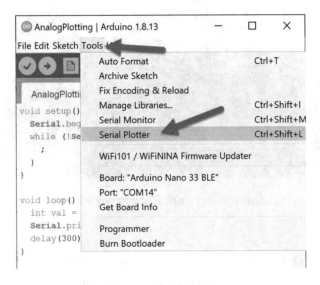

Figure 2-14. *Opening the Serial Plotter tool*

After you select Serial Plotter, you will see the dialog box shown in Figure 2-15. Make noise into the SparkFun Electret Microphone Breakout to obtain various signals on the plotter tool. Because we use delay(300), the plotter updates its graphs every 300 ms.

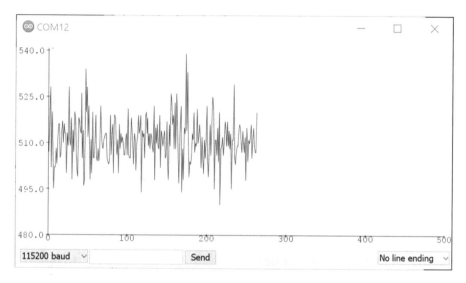

Figure 2-15. *Plotting sensor sound data*

How does this work? It is very simple. First, read an analog sensor by calling analogRead().

```
void loop() {
  int val = analogRead(A0);
```

Then, print to the serial terminal using println() from the Serial object.

```
  Serial.println(val);
  delay(300);
```

This prompts Serial Plotter to display a graph.

Serial Communication

Serial communication is the process of sending data one bit at a time, sequentially, over a communication channel. In Arduino Nano 33 BLE Sense, we can implement serial communication using the Serial object. We already used this Serial object in previous projects to show program output using Serial Monitor.

You can write data into serial communication by calling print() and println() from the Serial object. For further information about the Serial object, visit https://www.arduino.cc/reference/en/language/functions/communication/serial/.

This demonstration builds a blink program. Each LED state is written into the serial terminal. Use a baud rate setting of 115200. You can open the Arduino software and write this complete program.

```
int led = 13;

void setup() {
  Serial.begin(115200);
  pinMode(led, OUTPUT);
}

void loop() {
  Serial.println("LED: HIGH");
  digitalWrite(led, HIGH);
  delay(1000);
  Serial.println("LED: LOW");
  digitalWrite(led, LOW);
  delay(1000);
}
```

Save this program as SerialDemo, then compile and upload this program into the Arduino Nano 33 BLE Sense. Open Serial Monitor to view the program output, as displayed in Figure 2-16.

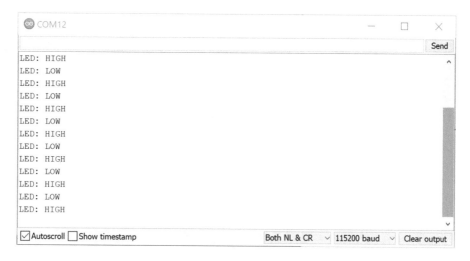

Figure 2-16. *Program output for SerialDemo program*

Pulse-Width Modulation

PWM is a method to control analog output. Technically, it is not "true" analog output. Microcontroller Unit (MCU) can manipulate the duty cycle to generate pulses. Arduino Nano 33 BLE Sense has PWM pins on all digital pins. You can see a ~ sign the on digital pins that are PWM pins. Refer to Figure 2-9, which shows digital pins, such as D2~. In general, Arduino Nano 33 BLE Sense has 14 PWM pins on digital pins: 0, 1, 2, 3, 4, 5, 6, 7, 8, 9, 10, 11, 12, 13.

For this demonstration, we use an RGB LED. This LED has four pins. Three pins are the red, green, and blue pins. The rest could be GND or VCC, depending on the RGB cathode or anode model. You can implement the following wiring for this example, which is shown in Figure 2-17.

- RGB red pin is connected to Arduino digital pin 12.

- RGB green pin is connected to Arduino digital pin 11.

- RGB blue pin is connected to Arduino digital pin 10.

- RGB GND pin is connected to Arduino digital pin GND.

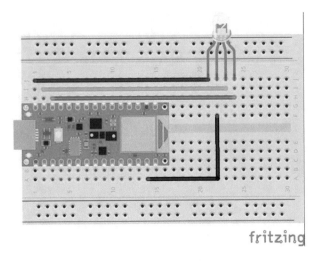

Figure 2-17. Wiring for Arduino and RGB LED

Now you can create an Arduino program to generate some colors with the RGB LED: red, green, blue, yellow, purple, and aqua. Open the Arduino software and write this complete program.

```
int redPin = 12;
int greenPin = 11;
int bluePin = 10;

void setup()
{
    pinMode(redPin, OUTPUT);
    pinMode(greenPin, OUTPUT);
    pinMode(bluePin, OUTPUT);
    Serial.begin(115200);
}

void loop()
{
  setColor(255, 0, 0);  // red
  Serial.println("red");
```

```
  delay(1000);
  setColor(0, 255, 0);  // green
  Serial.println("green");
  delay(1000);
  setColor(0, 0, 255);  // blue
  Serial.println("blue");
  delay(1000);
  setColor(255, 255, 0);  // yellow
  Serial.println("yellow");
  delay(1000);
  setColor(80, 0, 80);  // purple
  Serial.println("purple");
  delay(1000);
  setColor(0, 255, 255);  // aqua
  Serial.println("aqua");
  delay(1000);
}

void setColor(int red, int green, int blue)
{
  analogWrite(redPin, red);
  analogWrite(greenPin, green);
  analogWrite(bluePin, blue);
}
```

Save this program as test_rgb_arduino, then compile and upload this program into the Arduino Nano 33 BLE Sense. You should see some colors on the RGB LED. You also can open Serial Monitor to see the program output, which is also displayed in Figure 2-18.

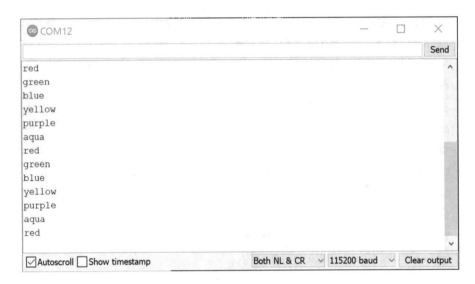

Figure 2-18. *Program output for RGB application*

How does this work? Initialize the digital pins for PWM pins. Call pinMode() with OUTPUT mode. You also also configure the Serial object with a baud rate value of 115200.

```
int redPin = 12;
int greenPin = 11;
int bluePin = 10;

void setup()
{
    pinMode(redPin, OUTPUT);
    pinMode(greenPin, OUTPUT);
    pinMode(bluePin, OUTPUT);
    Serial.begin(115200);
}
```

Next, define the setColor() function to generate a color from combining red, green, and blue color values. Call analogWrite() to write data for PWM data.

```
void setColor(int red, int green, int blue)
{
  analogWrite(redPin, red);
  analogWrite(greenPin, green);
  analogWrite(bluePin, blue);
}
```

Next, generate some colors on the loop() function. For instance, we want to set Red = 255, Green = 0, and Blue = 0. These samples generate color for red, green, and blue.

```
void loop()
{
  setColor(255, 0, 0);  // red
  Serial.println("red");
  delay(1000);
  setColor(0, 255, 0);  // green
  Serial.println("green");
  delay(1000);
  setColor(0, 0, 255);  // blue
  Serial.println("blue");
  delay(1000);
```

You can also generate colors for yellow, purple, and aqua by inserting values for red, green, and blue.

```
  setColor(255, 255, 0);  // yellow
  Serial.println("yellow");
  delay(1000);
  setColor(80, 0, 80);  // purple
  Serial.println("purple");
  delay(1000);
  setColor(0, 255, 255);  // aqua
  Serial.println("aqua");
  delay(1000);
```

You can practice generating new colors by combining different values for red, green, and blue. Values can be set from 0 to 255.

Serial Peripheral Interface

Serial communication works with asynchronous mode so there is no control on serial communication. This means we cannot guarantee the data that are sent will be received by the intended receiver. SPI is a synchronous serial communication interface specification, but SPI has four wires to control data such as MOSI, MISO, SCLK, and SS.

Arduino Nano 33 BLE Sense has one SPI interface with the following SPI pins.

- MOSI on digital pin 11.

- MISO on digital pin 12.

- SCLK on digital pin 13.

You can attach any sensor or actuator-based SPI interface to the Arduino Nano 33 BLE Sense board. For this example, we only connect the MISO pin to the MOSI pin using a jumper cable. You can connect digital pin 12 to digital pin 11. Figure 2-19 shows the wiring for this SPI demo.

Figure 2-19. *Connecting MISO and MOSI pins from Arduino SPI*

To access the SPI interface on Arduino Nano 33 BLE Sense, you can use the SPI library. Detailed information about this library is available at https://www.arduino.cc/en/Reference/SPI.

Now we can build an Arduino program. This program will send data to and receive data from SPI. To begin, open the Arduino software and then write this complete program.

```
#include <SPI.h>

byte sendData,recvData;
void setup() {
  SPI.begin();
```

```
  Serial.begin(9600);
  randomSeed(80);
}
void loop() {
  sendData = random(50, 100);
  recvData = SPI.transfer(sendData);

  Serial.print("Send=");
  Serial.println(sendData,DEC);
  Serial.print("Recv=");
  Serial.println(recvData,DEC);
  delay(800);
}
```

Save this program as SPIDemo, then compile and upload this program into the Arduino Nano 33 BLE Sense. You can open Serial Monitor to see the program output, which is also shown in Figure 2-20.

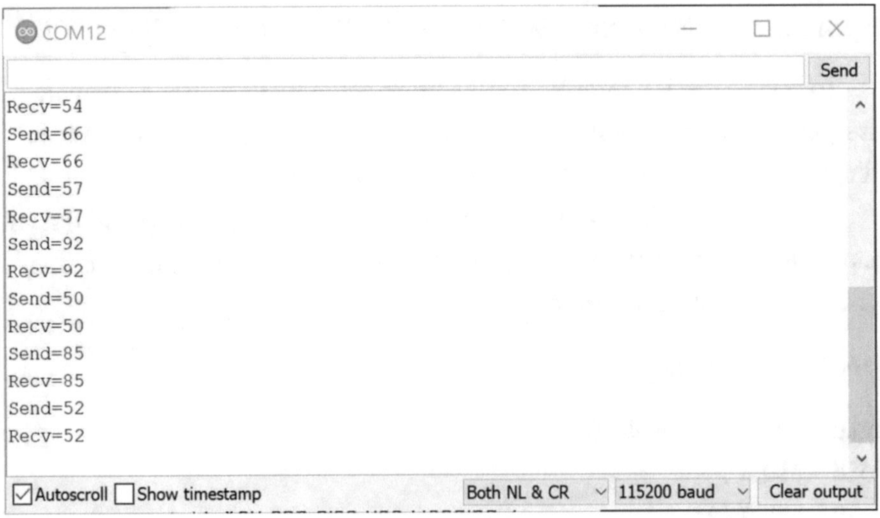

Figure 2-20. *Program output for SPI program*

How does this work? First, initialize SPI and the Serial interface on setup() function.

```
#include <SPI.h>

byte sendData,recvData;
void setup() {
  SPI.begin();
  Serial.begin(9600);
  randomSeed(80);
}
```

To send and receive data over SPI, you can use the SPI.transfer() function. You can send data with random values in the loop() function.

```
void loop() {
  sendData = random(50, 100);
  recvData = SPI.transfer(sendData);
```

Next, print the sent and received data on the serial terminal.

```
  Serial.print("Send=");
  Serial.println(sendData,DEC);
  Serial.print("Recv=");
  Serial.println(recvData,DEC);
```

That complete the SPI demo. You can practice further by applying sensor and actuator devices.

Inter-Integrated Circuit

The Inter-Integrated Circuit (I2C) protocol is a protocol intended to allow multiple "slave" modules or devices (chips) to communicate with one or more "master" chips. This protocol works with asynchronous mode. To communicate with other devices or modules, the I2C protocol defines I2C addresses for all slave devices.

The I2C interface has two pins: SDA and SCL. For data transfer, the I2C interface uses the SDA pin. The SCL pin is used for clocking. The Arduino Nano 33 BLE Sense board has I2C pins on A4 as SDA and A5 as SCL.

For this example, we use a sensor-module-based I2C interface. The I2C interface uses a device address so the Arduino Nano 33 BLE Sense board can access data by opening a connection to the I2C address. Each analog sensor from the sensor-module-based I2C will be attached to an I2C address.

For testing in this example, an PCF8591 AD/DA Converter module with sensor and actuator devices is used, as shown in Figure 2-21. The PCF8591 AD/DA module uses a PCF8591 chip that consists of four analog inputs and an AD converter. The PCF8591 chip also has analog output with a DA converter. For further information about the PCF8591 chip, see `https://www.nxp.com/products/interfaces/ic-spi-serial-interface-devices/ic-dacs-and-adcs/8-bit-a-d-and-d-a-converter:PCF8591`. This type of module can be purchased online or at your local store.

Figure 2-21. *PCF8591 ADC DAC AD/DA module*

Based on the documentation for the PCF8591 AD/DA Converter module, this module uses an I2C address on 0x48. The PCF8591 AD/DA Converter module also consists of three sensors.

- Thermistor: Using channel 0.

- Photoresistor: Using channel 1.

- Potentiometer: Using channel 3.

Now Attaching PCF8591 AD/DA Converter module to Arduino Nano 33 BLE Sense board with the following wiring.

- PCF8591 AD/DA module SDA is connected to Arduino A4 pin.

- PCF8591 AD/DA module SCL is connected to Arduino A5 pin.

- PCF8591 AD/DA module VCC is connected to Arduino 3.3V.

- PCF8591 AD/DA module GND is connected to Arduino GND pin.

Figure 2-22 shows wiring for the PCF8591 AD/DA Converter module and Arduino Nano 33 BLE Sense board. You should see a lighted LED when you plug in 3.3V to the module.

Figure 2-22. *Wiring PCF8591 ADC DAC AD/DA module with Arduino Nano 33 BLE Sense*

Now that we have finished our wiring for this demonstration, we can implement two project demos: an I2C scanning application and an I2C sensor application. First, let's build a scanning I2C address application on the Arduino Nano 33 BLE Sense board.

Scanning I2C Address

Every device or module-based-I2C set has its own I2C address on MCU. In this section, we want to scan all devices that are attached on the Arduino Nano 33 BLE Sense. We also have some internal sensor devices based on I2C inside the Arduino Nano 33 BLE Sense.

To access I2C on the Arduino board, you can use Wire library. We can include our program by inserting the `wire.h` library. For more information about the Wire library, consult the official Arduino website at `https://www.arduino.cc/en/Reference/Wire`.

This demo uses the wiring demo from the PCF8591 AD/DA Converter module shown previously in Figure 2-22. This program was modified from `https://playground.arduino.cc/Main/I2cScanner/`. Open the Arduino software and write this complete program.

```
#include <Wire.h>

void setup() {

  Serial.begin(115200);
  Wire.begin();
  Serial.println("\nI2C Scanner");
}

void loop() {
  byte error, address;
  int nDevices;

  Serial.println("Scanning...");

  nDevices = 0;
  for(address = 1; address < 127; address++) {
    Wire.beginTransmission(address);
    error = Wire.endTransmission();
```

```
    if (error == 0) {
      Serial.print("I2C device found at address 0x");
      if (address < 16)
        Serial.print("0");
      Serial.println(address, HEX);

      nDevices++;
    }
    else if (error == 4) {
      Serial.print("Unknown error at address 0x");
      if (address < 16)
        Serial.print("0");
      Serial.println(address, HEX);
    }
  }
  if (nDevices == 0)
    Serial.println("No I2C devices found");
  else
    Serial.println("done");

  delay(5000);
}
```

Save this program as i2c_scanner. You can then compile and upload this program into the Arduino Nano 33 BLE Sense. You can view the program output using Serial Monitor, as displayed in Figure 2-23. You can see that there are three I2C addresses. 0x48 is our PCF8591 AD/DA Converter module, and two I2C addresses, 0x51 and 0x55, are internal I2C sensors inside the Arduino Nano 33 BLE Sense.

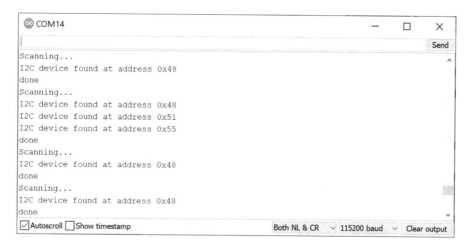

Figure 2-23. *Program output for reading I2C address*

How does this work? First, initialize the I2C and serial interfaces in the setup() function. Set the baud rate serial value to 115200.

```
#include <Wire.h>

void setup() {

  Serial.begin(115200);
  Wire.begin();
  Serial.println("\nI2C Scanner");
}
```

In the loop() function, we perform a scan for the I2C address by probing I2C data. Set initialize nDevices = 0 for the number of I2C devices to find. Perform a looping task from address 0 to 127.

Next, open the I2C interface using Wire.beginTransmission(), then close a transmission by calling wire.endTransmission().

```
nDevices = 0;
  for(address = 1; address < 127; address++) {
    Wire.beginTransmission(address);
    error = Wire.endTransmission();
```

Check for value error. If there is no error, it means you have an I2C device on the current address. Print the I2C address to the serial terminal using `Serial.println()` with HEX mode.

```
  if (error == 0) {
    Serial.print("I2C device found at address 0x");
    if (address < 16)
      Serial.print("0");
    Serial.println(address, HEX);

    nDevices++;
  }
```

Otherwise, check the error code. If `error = 4`, we print errors on this address for unknown errors on the current address.

```
  else if (error == 4) {
    Serial.print("Unknown error at address 0x");
    if (address < 16)
      Serial.print("0");
    Serial.println(address, HEX);
  }
```

Finally, print the findings on the I2C interface on the serial terminal.

```
  if (nDevices == 0)
    Serial.println("No I2C devices found");
  else
    Serial.println("done");
```

This program is useful to check a list of I2C devices that is attached on the Arduino Nano 33 BLE Sense board.

Reading Sensor-Based-I2C Addresses

In this section, we read sensor data from an I2C device. You already configured the hardware wiring shown in Figure 2-22. The PCF8591 AD/DA Converter module has three sensors: thermistor, photo-voltaic cell, and potentiometer. Each sensor has a channel address on 0x00, 0x01, and 0x03, respectively.

Let's start to build an Arduino program to access sensor devices over the I2C interface. Open the Arduino software and write this complete program.

```
#include "Wire.h"
#define PCF8591 0x48 // I2C bus address
#define PCF8591_ADC_CH0 0x00 // thermistor
#define PCF8591_ADC_CH1 0x01 // photo-voltaic cell
#define PCF8591_ADC_CH2 0x02
#define PCF8591_ADC_CH3 0x03 // potentiometer
byte ADC1, ADC2, ADC3;

void setup()
{
  Wire.begin();
  Serial.begin(9600);
}
void loop()
{
  // read thermistor
  Wire.beginTransmission(PCF8591);
  Wire.write((byte)PCF8591_ADC_CH0);
  Wire.endTransmission();
  delay(100);
  Wire.requestFrom(PCF8591, 2);
```

```
delay(100);
ADC1=Wire.read();
ADC1=Wire.read();

Serial.print("Thermistor=");
Serial.println(ADC1);

// read photo-voltaic cell
Wire.beginTransmission(PCF8591);
Wire.write(PCF8591_ADC_CH1);
Wire.endTransmission();
delay(100);
Wire.requestFrom(PCF8591, 2);
delay(100);
ADC2=Wire.read();
ADC2=Wire.read();

Serial.print("Photo-voltaic cell=");
Serial.println(ADC2);

// potentiometer
Wire.beginTransmission(PCF8591);
Wire.write(PCF8591_ADC_CH3);
Wire.endTransmission();
delay(100);
Wire.requestFrom(PCF8591, 2);
delay(100);
ADC3=Wire.read();
ADC3=Wire.read();

Serial.print("potentiometer=");
Serial.println(ADC3);

delay(500);
}
```

Save this program as I2CSensor. Next you can compile and upload this program into the Arduino Nano 33 BLE Sense. Open Serial Monitor on the Arduino software to view the sensor data from the I2C protocol, as shown in Figure 2-24.

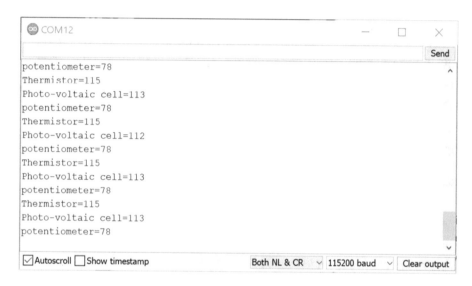

Figure 2-24. *Program output for reading sensors over I2C*

How does it work? First, initialize your I2C, Serial, and PCF8591 AD/ DA Converter module. Define the I2C address channel in the setup() function.

```
#include "Wire.h"
#define PCF8591 0x48 // I2C bus address
#define PCF8591_ADC_CH0 0x00 // thermistor
#define PCF8591_ADC_CH1 0x01 // photo-voltaic cell
#define PCF8591_ADC_CH2 0x02
#define PCF8591_ADC_CH3 0x03 // potentiometer
byte ADC1, ADC2, ADC3;
```

```
void setup()
{
  Wire.begin();
  Serial.begin(9600);
}
```

You can read sensor data in the loop() function. To read thermistor data, open I2C using Wire.beginTransmission() with passing PCF8591. Then, select a channel for the thermistor with the value PCF8591_ADC_CH0 using Wire.write(). Close transmission by calling Wire.endTransmission(). Read sensor data with 2 bytes using the Wire.requestFrom() function.

```
void loop()
{
  // read thermistor
  Wire.beginTransmission(PCF8591);
  Wire.write((byte)PCF8591_ADC_CH0);
  Wire.endTransmission();
  delay(100);
  Wire.requestFrom(PCF8591, 2);
  delay(100);
  ADC1=Wire.read();
  ADC1=Wire.read();
```

Set delay(100) to wait for the module to complete your request. You can read data per byte using the Wire.read() function. Next, print the thermistor data on the serial terminal.

```
  Serial.print("Thermistor=");
  Serial.println(ADC1);
```

With the same method, you can read the photo-voltaic cell by changing the channel value to PCF8591_ADC_CH1. After that, read sensor data and print the results to the serial terminal.

```
// read photo-voltaic cell
Wire.beginTransmission(PCF8591);
Wire.write(PCF8591_ADC_CH1);
Wire.endTransmission();
delay(100);
Wire.requestFrom(PCF8591, 2);
delay(100);
ADC2=Wire.read();
ADC2=Wire.read();

Serial.print("Photo-voltaic cell=");
Serial.println(ADC2);
```

You can also read the potentiometer from the PCF8591 AD/DA Converter module. Open the I2C interface and select the channel for PCF8591_ADC_CH3. Then, you can read sensor data and print it on the serial terminal.

```
// potentiometer
Wire.beginTransmission(PCF8591);
Wire.write(PCF8591_ADC_CH3);
Wire.endTransmission();
delay(100);
Wire.requestFrom(PCF8591, 2);
delay(100);
ADC3=Wire.read();
ADC3=Wire.read();

Serial.print("potentiometer=");
Serial.println(ADC3);
```

You can continue your practice on the Arduino Nano 33 BLE Sense with some of the protocols that we have already learned.

Summary

This chapter covered basic Arduino programming using Sketch. You learned how to access digital and analog I/O on the Arduino Nano 33 BLE Sense board. We also explored how to implement PWM on Arduino Nano 33 BLE Sense and plot sensor data. Furthermore, you learned to use SPI and I2C interfaces to communicate with external devices.

Next, we explore how to access internal sensor devices on the Arduino Nano 33 BLE Sense.

CHAPTER 3

Sensor Programming

The Arduino Nano 33 BLE Sense board has some internal sensors such as an inertial measurement unit (IMU), a pressure sensor, a digital microphone, a humidity and temperature sensor, and a gesture sensor. This chapter explores how to access internal sensor devices on the Arduino Nano 33 BLE Sense.

You will learn about the following topics in this chapter:

- Accessing the temperature and relative humidity sensor.

- Plotting sensor data.

- Plotting sensor data using an OLED I2C display.

- Accessing the IMU sensor.

- Accessing the pressure sensor.

- Working with a digital microphone.

- Working with a gesture sensor.

© Agus Kurniawan 2021
A. Kurniawan, *IoT Projects with Arduino Nano 33 BLE Sense*,
https://doi.org/10.1007/978-1-4842-6458-4_3

Introduction

The Arduino Nano 33 BLE Sense board has some internal sensors such as IMU, a pressure sensor, a digital microphone, a humidity and temperature sensor, and a gesture sensor. These sensor chips are shown in Figure 3-1. Most sensor chips are attached on I2C protocol interfaces.

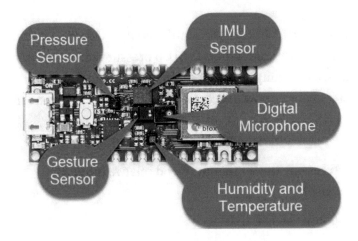

Figure 3-1. *Some sensor chips on the Arduino Nano 33 BLE Sense board*

In Chapter 2, we learned about the I2C interface. We also performed a scan for the I2C address. We can modify the i2c_scanner program from Chapter 2 to list all I2C addresses in the Arduino Nano 33 BLE Sense. You can write these complete scripts.

```
#include <Wire.h>

void setup() {
  Serial.begin(115200);
  Wire.begin();
  Serial.println("\nI2C Scanner");
}
```

```
void loop() {
  byte error, address;

  int nDevices;
  nDevices = 0;
  for(address = 1; address < 127; address++) {
    Wire.beginTransmission(address);
    error = Wire.endTransmission();

    if (error == 0) {
      Serial.print("I2C device found at address 0x");
      if (address < 16)
        Serial.print("0");
      Serial.println(address, HEX);

      nDevices++;
    }
  }
  delay(5000);
}
```

Save this program as i2c_internalsensor. Next, compile and upload this program into the Arduino Nano 33 BLE Sense. Make sure to change your board position, shake your board, or move your board so you have a measurement result on the serial terminal.

Figure 3-2 shows the program output for the i2c_internalsensor program, a list of I2C addresses in the Arduino Nano 33 BLE Sense.

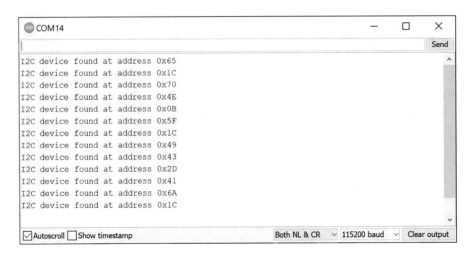

Figure 3-2. *A list of I2C address in the Arduino Nano 33 BLE Sense*

Temperature and Relative Humidity

The Arduino Nano 33 BLE Sense board has a built-in temperature and relative humidity sensor that uses HTS221. To work with this sensor, use the Arduino_HTS221 library. You can documentation for this sensor at `https://www.arduino.cc/en/Reference/ArduinoHTS221`.

You can install the Arduino_HTS221 library via Library Manager. Type Arduino_HTS221 in the search text box so you can see the Arduino_HTS221 library, as shown in Figure 3-3.

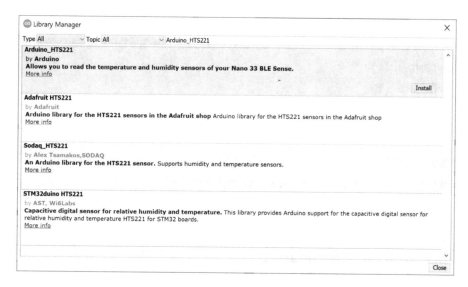

Figure 3-3. *Installing the Arduino_HTS221 library*

Click Install to install the Arduino_HTS221 library. Make sure your computer has Internet access. After that, you can access the HTS221 sensor.

For this demonstration, we read the temperature and relative humidity sensor. You can use the `readTemperature()` function from the HTS object to read temperature. You can also can call the `readHumidity()` function to read humidity. Before you call these functions, initialize the sensor device by calling the `HTS.begin()` function. Finaly, you can print the sensor data into the serial terminal.

Open the Arduino software and write these scripts to read the temperature and humidity sensors.

```
#include <Arduino_HTS221.h>

void setup() {
  Serial.begin(115200);
  while (!Serial);
```

```
  if (!HTS.begin()) {
    Serial.println("Failed to initialize humidity temperature
    sensor!");
    while (1);
  }
}

void loop() {
  float temperature = HTS.readTemperature();
  float humidity    = HTS.readHumidity();

  Serial.print("Temperature = ");
  Serial.print(temperature);
  Serial.println(" °C");

  Serial.print("Humidity    = ");
  Serial.print(humidity);
  Serial.println(" %");

  Serial.println();
  delay(1000);
}
```

Save this program as TempHumidity. You can then compile and upload this program into the Arduino Nano 33 BLE Sense. We can the see program output using Serial Monitor, as shown in Figure 3-4.

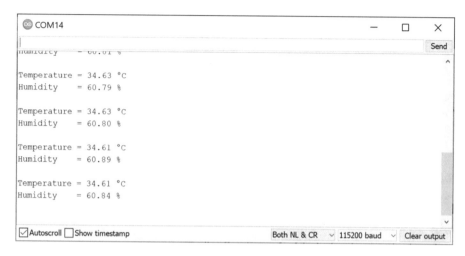

Figure 3-4. *Program output for TempHumidity program*

Plotting Sensor Data

You just saw that we can read temperature and humidity sensor data from built-in sensor devices on the Arduino Nano 33 BLE Sense. In this section, we plot our sensor data using the Serial Plotter tool from Arduino. For testing, use the preceding project that reads temperature and humidity sensors.

The first step is to create a new Sketch program. Open the Arduino software and include the HTS221 library in the program. Next, initialize the HTS221 sensor and serial communication in the setup() function. Set the serial baud rate value to 115200 and initialize HTS221 by calling the HTS. begin() function.

```
#include <Arduino_HTS221.h>

void setup() {
  Serial.begin(115200);
  while (!Serial);
```

```
  if (!HTS.begin()) {
    Serial.println("Failed to initialize humidity temperature
    sensor!");
    while (1);
  }
}
```

In the loop() function, we read the temperature sensor using HTS.readTemperature(). We also read the humidity sensor using the HTS.readHumidity() function.

```
void loop() {
  float temperature = HTS.readTemperature();
  float humidity    = HTS.readHumidity();
```

To plot the temperature and humidity sensors to Serial Plotter, you can print sensor values with the , delimiter. To set a legend name on Serial Plotter, you can use "sensor_name:". For instance, you can print the temperature and humidity sensor variables as follows.

```
  Serial.print("Temperature:");
  Serial.print(temperature);
  Serial.print(", ");
  Serial.print("Humidity:");
  Serial.println(humidity);
  delay(500);
}
```

Now save this program as Plot_TempHumidity. You can then compile and upload the program into the Arduino Nano 33 BLE Sense. After uploading the program, open Serial Plotter from Tools menu in the Arduino software. You should see the sensor outputs in Serial Plotter, too. Figure 3-5 shows the program output from the Plot_TempHumidity program. You also should see the sensor legend names like Temperature and Humidity.

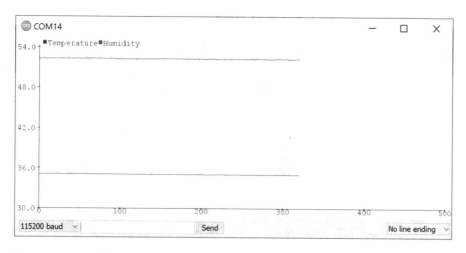

Figure 3-5. *Plotting the Plot_TempHumidity sensor data in Serial Plotter*

Plotting Sensor Data Using an OLED I2C Display

In this section, we cover how to display sensor data on an OLED display. There are two interface models on an OLED display: SPI and I2C. This demonstration uses an OLED I2C display that you can buy at any local electronics store or online.

For this demo, I used an OLED I2C display with 0.96 inch or 128 × 64 pixels, obtained online and shown in Figure 3-6. Technically, you can use any display size for the OLE I2C display. The next step is wiring OLED I2C display to the Arduino Nano 33 BLE Sense board.

Figure 3-6. OLED 0.96" I2C display

Wiring for the OLED I2C Display

We use an OLED display with an I2C interface so we can connect the
display to the Arduino Nano 33 BLE Sense over I2C pins. You can see
how the wiring should look in Figure 3-7. You can perform this wiring as
follows.

- OLED I2C display module SDA is connected to Arduino
  A4 pin.

- OLED I2C display module SCL is connected to Arduino
  A5 pin.

- OLED I2C display module VCC is connected to Arduino
  3.3V.

- OLED I2C display module GND is connected to
  Arduino GND pin.

Figure 3-7. *Wiring the OLED I2C display on the Arduino Nano 33 BLE Sense*

Next, you can build an Arduino program for the OLED I2C display.

Checking the I2C Address of the OLED I2C Display

Now that the wiring between the Arduino Nano 33 BLE Sense and OLED I2C display is complete, you can use the i2c_scanner program from Chapter 2 to check for I2C addresses from devices. This will give you the I2C address from the OLED I2C display.

Load the i2c_scanner program into the Arduino software, then compile and upload this program into the Arduino Nano 33 BLE Sense. After that, open Serial Monitor. You should see three I2C addresses. Two of them are

I2C built-in sensors on the Arduino Nano 33 BLE Sense. The third one is the OLED I2C display. The program output is shown in Figure 3-8. You can see the OLED I2C display running on the 0x3C I2C address.

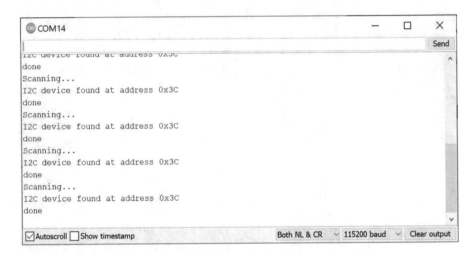

Figure 3-8.   *Detecting the I2C address for the OLED I2C display*

The next step is to set up libraries to build programs for the OLED I2C display on the Arduino Nano 33 BLE Sense.

Setting Up the OLED I2C Display Library

To work with the OLED I2C display on Arduino, you need to install two libraries from Adafruit.

- Adafruit_SSD1306: `https://github.com/adafruit/Adafruit_SSD1306`

- Adafruit GFX Library: `https://github.com/adafruit/Adafruit-GFX-Library`

We can install these libraries via Library Manager on the Arduino software. Type Adafruit_SSD1306 and Adafruit GFX Library to locate and install these libraries. Figure 3-9 shows the Adafruit_SSD1306 library.

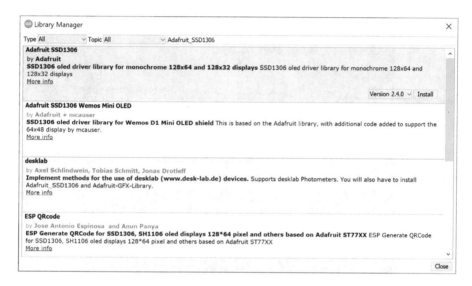

Figure 3-9. *Adding libraries for the OLED I2C display*

Install both of the libraries. You might be asked to install additional libraries (e.g., Adafruit BusIO) to enable working the with Adafruit_SSD1306 and Adafruit GFX libraries.

Testing the OLED I2C Display

After the Adafruit_SSD1306 library is installed, you can test your OLED I2C display using program samples from the Adafruit_SSD1306 library. From the File menu, select Examples ➤ Adafruit_SSD1306 ➤ ssd1306_128x64_i2c. Once you make this selection, you should see the codes shown in Figure 3-10.

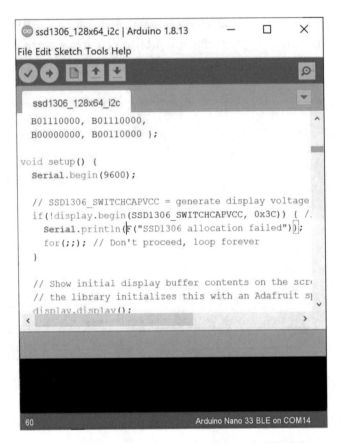

Figure 3-10. *A program sample for the OLED I2C display*

Next, modify this program with the I2C address from your OLED I2C display. In the previous section, we found the 0x3C address for the OLED I2C display. Replace the I2C address in display.begin() with 0x3C as shown in Figure 3-10.

Now you can compile and upload this program to the the Arduino Nano 33 BLE Sense. You should see some forms on the OLED I2C display. Figure 3-11 shows the program output from ssd1306_128x64_i2c on the OLED I2C display with 128 × 64 pixels.

Figure 3-11. *Running the ssd1306_128x64_i2c program on the OLED I2C display*

If you can see the display output from the ssd1306_128x64_i2c program, it means your OLED I2C display works. We will use this OLED to display sensor data in the following demonstrations. If you don't see the display output, first, check the I2C address of the OLED I2C display. Then, make sure your OLED I2C display has a display size of 128 × 64 pixels.

Displaying Temperature and Humidity Sensor

In this section, we build an Arduino program to display the output of the temperature and humidity data sensors to the OLED I2C display. You can use a program from the previous section to read the temperature and humidity sensor.

Open the Arduino software and create a new Sketch program. Start by importing all required libraries for the I2C library, OLED I2C display, and HTS221 sensor.

```
#include <SPI.h>
#include <Wire.h>
#include <Adafruit_GFX.h>
#include <Adafruit_SSD1306.h>
#include <Arduino_HTS221.h>
```

Next you need to define the OLED I2C display size. For this demo, I used 128 × 64 pixels. You can change the size based on your OLED module.

```
#define SCREEN_WIDTH 128
#define SCREEN_HEIGHT 64
```

Next, configure Adafruit_SSD1306 with the I2C address of the OLED module and display size.

```
#define OLED_RESET     4 // Reset pin
Adafruit_SSD1306 display(SCREEN_WIDTH, SCREEN_HEIGHT, &Wire,
OLED_RESET);
```

In the setup() function, initialize serial communication and the Adafruit_SSD1306 library. Call display.begin() with some parameters to initialize your OLED display.

```
void setup() {
  Serial.begin(115200);

  if(!display.begin(SSD1306_SWITCHCAPVCC, 0x3C)) {
    Serial.println(F("SSD1306 allocation failed"));
    for(;;); // Don't proceed, loop forever
  }
```

After that, test the OLED I2C display by calling display() for 2 seconds. Then, clear the screen of the OLED display.

```
display.display();
delay(2000); // Pause for 2 seconds

// Clear the buffer
display.clearDisplay();
```

Finally, initialize the HTS221 sensor by calling the HTS.begin() function.

```
if (!HTS.begin()) {
  Serial.println("Failed to initialize humidity temperature
  sensor!");
  while (1);
}
```

In the loop() function, read the temperature and humidity sensors. Call the HTS.readTemperature() function to read the temperature sensor and the HTS.readHumidity() function to read the humidity sensor. Store all sensor data in the temperature and humidity variables.

```
void loop() {
  float temperature = HTS.readTemperature();
  float humidity    = HTS.readHumidity();
```

Next, display the sensor data on the OLED I2C display using the print() function. Use setTextSize() to set the font size for the display text.

```
display.clearDisplay();
display.setTextSize(1);
display.setTextColor(SSD1306_WHITE);
display.setCursor(0,0);
```

```
display.print("Temperature");
display.setTextSize(2);
display.setCursor(0,12);
String temp = String(temperature);
temp = temp + " *C";
display.print(temp);

display.setTextSize(1);
display.setCursor(0,30);
display.print("Humidity");
display.setTextSize(2);
display.setCursor(0,48);
display.print(String(humidity));
display.display();
```

Last, display the sensor data onto the serial terminal using the `Serial.print()` and `Serial.println()` functions.

```
Serial.print("Temperature = ");
Serial.print(temperature);
Serial.println(" °C");

Serial.print("Humidity     = ");
Serial.print(humidity);
Serial.println(" %");

Serial.println();
delay(1000);
}
```

Save the program as OledSensor, then compile and upload the program to the Arduino Nano 33 BLE Sense. You should see sensor data on the OLED I2C display, as shown in Figure 3-12. Figure 3-13 shows the program output on Serial Monitor.

Figure 3-12. *Displaying sensor data on an OLED I2C display*

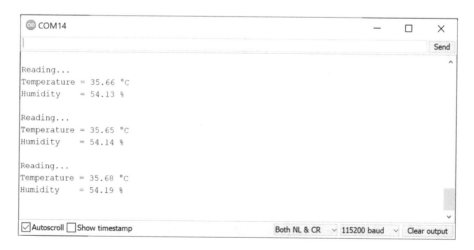

Figure 3-13. *Program output from OledSensor*

IMU Sensor

The Arduino Nano 33 BLE Sense board has an IMU sensor with an LSM9DS3 chip. This chip provides IMU sensors such as an accelerometer, a gyroscope, and a magnetometer. We can use the Arduino_LSM9DS3 library to access the IMU sensor on the Arduino Nano 33 BLE Sense. You can find this library at `https://www.arduino.cc/en/Reference/ArduinoLSM9DS1`.

To install the Arduino_LSM9DS3 library, use Library Manager and enter Arduino_LSM9DS3 in the search text box. You should see this library as shown in Figure 3-14. Install this library by clicking Install.

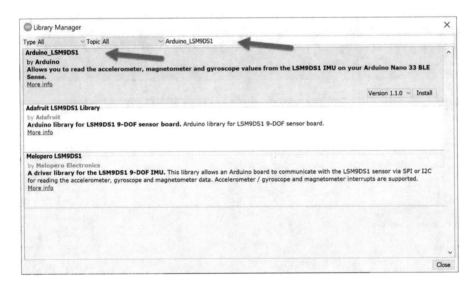

Figure 3-14. *Installing the Arduino_LSM9DS1 library*

The next step is to build a Sketch program to read the accelerometer, gyroscope, and magnetometer sensors on the Arduino Nano 33 BLE Sense. You need to open the Arduino software and create a new program. First, initialize serial communication and the Arduino_LSM9DS1 libraries in the setup() function.

```
#include <Arduino_LSM9DS1.h>

void setup() {
  Serial.begin(115200);
  while (!Serial);
  Serial.println("Started");

  if (!IMU.begin()) {
    Serial.println("Failed to initialize IMU!");
    while (1);
  }
}
```

In the loop() function, we read acceleration sensor. Check if sensor data are available using IMU.accelerationAvailable(). Then, we can read sensor data by calling IMU.readAcceleration(). After that, we print sensor data to serial terminal.

```
void loop() {
  float x, y, z;

  if (IMU.accelerationAvailable()) {
    IMU.readAcceleration(x, y, z);

    Serial.print("Accelerometer: ");
    Serial.print(x);
    Serial.print('\t');
    Serial.print(y);
    Serial.print('\t');
    Serial.println(z);
  }
```

Next, read the gyroscope sensor by calling IMU.readGyroscope() after calling the IMU.gyroscopeAvailable() function.

```
if (IMU.gyroscopeAvailable()) {
  IMU.readGyroscope(x, y, z);

  Serial.print("Gyroscop: ");
  Serial.print(x);
  Serial.print('\t');
  Serial.print(y);
  Serial.print('\t');
  Serial.println(z);
}
```

Last, we read a magnetic field sensor on the Arduino Nano 33 BLE
Sense by calling the IMU.readMagneticField() function and then
print the result to the serial terminal. Make sure you call the IMU.
gyroscopeAvailable() function before reading the sensor data.

```
if (IMU.magneticFieldAvailable()) {
  IMU.readMagneticField(x, y, z);

  Serial.print("Magnetic Field: ");
  Serial.print(x);
  Serial.print('\t');
  Serial.print(y);
  Serial.print('\t');
  Serial.println(z);
}

  delay(300);
}
```

Save this program as IMUSensor, then compile and upload it to
the Arduino Nano 33 BLE Sense. You can see program output on Serial
Monitor, as shown in Figure 3-15.

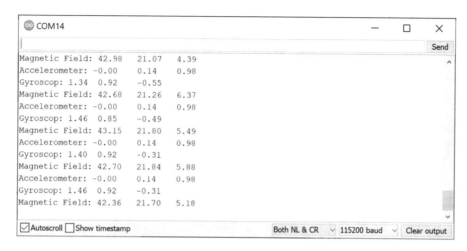

Figure 3-15. *Program output from IMUSensor program*

Pressure Sensor

The Arduino Nano 33 BLE Sense has a pressure sensor with an LPS22HIB chip. This chip provides a pressure sensor with values ranging from 260 to 1260 hPa. In this section, we access the pressure sensor on the Arduino Nano 33 BLE Sense.

We can use the Arduino_LPS22HB library to access pressure sensor on the Arduino Nano 33 BLE Sense board. You can find this library at https://www.arduino.cc/en/Reference/ArduinoLPS22HB.

To access the pressure sensor, install the Arduino_LPS22HB library in Library Manager. You can type Arduino_LPS22HB in the search text box to displays the library, as shown in Figure 3-16. Click Install to install the library.

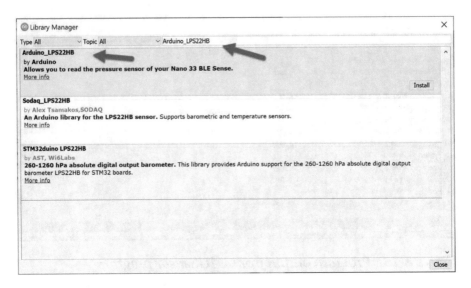

Figure 3-16. *Installing the Arduino_LPS22HB library*

The next step is to write a Sketch program to read the pressure data on the Arduino Nano 33 BLE Sense.

Open the Arduino software. We can access the pressure sensor using the Arduino_LPS22HB library. First, initialize the LPS22HB chip in the setup() function by calling the BARO.begin() function.

```
#include <Arduino_LPS22HB.h>

void setup() {
  Serial.begin(115200);
  while (!Serial);

  if (!BARO.begin()) {
    Serial.println("Failed to initialize pressure sensor!");
    while (1);
  }
}
```

In the loop() function, read the pressure sensor data by calling the BARO.readPressure() function. You can then print the sensor data to the serial terminal.

```
void loop() {
  float pressure = BARO.readPressure();

  Serial.print("Pressure: ");
  Serial.print(pressure);
  Serial.println(" kPa");

  delay(1000);
}
```

Save this program as PressureSensor, then compile and upload it to the Arduino Nano 33 BLE Sense. You can see the program output in Serial Monitor, as displayed in Figure 3-17.

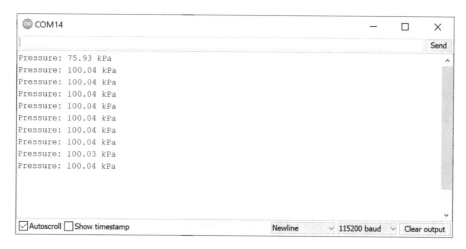

Figure 3-17. *Program output from PressureSensor*

Digital Microphone

The Arduino Nano 33 BLE Sense board provides a digital microphone.
Refer back to Figure 3-1 to see the microphone position. This digital
microphone is built from MP34DT06JTR. To work with a digital
microphone on Arduino Nano 33 BLE Sense, use the PDM library. This
library is installed when you install the Arduino Nano 33 BLE Sense board
with the Arduino software. The PDM library document can be read at
https://www.arduino.cc/en/Reference/PDM. For this demonstration, we
plot the amplitude value from the digital microphone using Serial Plotter.
You can open the Arduino software to start to write a program.

First, include the PDM library. Then declare the sampleBuffer variable
and samplesRead function.

```
#include <PDM.h>

short sampleBuffer[256];
// number of samples read
volatile int samplesRead;
```

In the setup() function, initialize serial communication. Pass the
onPDMdata() function to PDM.onReceive(). Then call PDM.begin() to
initialize the PDM library.

```
void setup() {
  Serial.begin(9600);
  while (!Serial);

  // configure the data receive callback
  PDM.onReceive(onPDMdata);

  // one channel (mono mode) 16 kHz sample rate
  if (!PDM.begin(1, 16000)) {
```

```
    Serial.println("Failed to start PDM!");
    while (1);
  }
}
```

In the loop() function, check the samplesRead value. If the samplesRead value is more than 1, we read sensor data from sampleBuffer[]. Then, print the data to the serial terminal.

```
void loop() {
  if (samplesRead) {
    for (int i = 0; i < samplesRead; i++) {
      Serial.println(sampleBuffer[i]);
    }

    // clear the read count
    samplesRead = 0;
  }
}
```

Implement the onPDMdata() function to read data from the digital microphone. We check if the data are available using the PDM.available() function. Then, read the sensor data by calling the PDM.read() function. This function is used by passing it to the PDM.onReceive() function. We already called it in the setup() function.

```
void onPDMdata() {
  // query the number of bytes available
  int bytesAvailable = PDM.available();

  // read into the sample buffer
  PDM.read(sampleBuffer, bytesAvailable);

  // 16-bit, 2 bytes per sample
  samplesRead = bytesAvailable / 2;
}
```

Save this program as PDMSerialPlotter. You can then compile and upload the program to the Arduino Nano 33 BLE Sense. You can see the program output on Serial Plotter. If you speak into the digital microphone from Arduino Nano 33 BLE Sense, you should see a signal graph on Serial Plotter, as displayed in Figure 3-18.

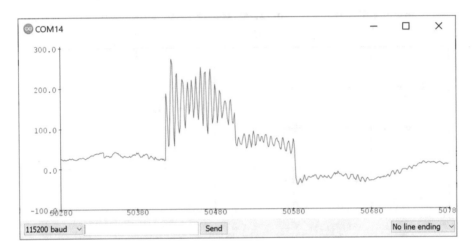

Figure 3-18. *Plotting amplitude values from a digital microphone*

Digital Proximity, Ambient Light, RGB, and Gesture Sensor

The Arduino Nano 33 BLE Sense has a special built-in sensor for digital proximity, ambient light, RGB color, and gesture sensors. These sensors use an APDS9960 chip, so we can include these sensors into our Sketch program. In this section, we explore all of the sensors inside the APDS9960 chip.

To work with the APDS9960 sensor chip, we can install the Arduino_ APDS9960 library via Library Manager. Type Arduino_APDS9960 in the search text box. You should see this library as shown in Figure 3-19. Click Install to install the library.

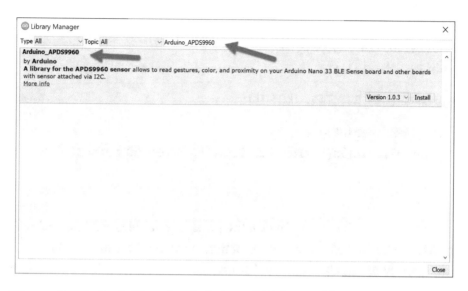

Figure 3-19. *Installing the Arduino_APDS9960 library*

Once the Arduino_APDS9960 library is installed, you can build various Sketch programs using the sensors from the APDS9960 chip. Detail about the Arduino_APDS9960 library found at https://www.arduino.cc/en/ Reference/ArduinoAPDS9960.

First, we build Sketch programs with the proximity sensor.

Proximity Sensor

The proximity sensor can be used to check for the existence of an object. When we put our object next to the APDS9960 chip, we will obtain a proximity value. This value can range from 0 to 255. For this demonstration, we build a program to turn on an LED when the proximity value is between 0 and 50.

Open the Arduino software to create a new program. First, initialize serial communication in the setup() function, digital mode for output, and Arduino_APDS9960 by calling the APDS.begin() function.

```
#include <Arduino_APDS9960.h>
```

```
void setup() {
  Serial.begin(115200);
  while (!Serial);

  pinMode(LED_BUILTIN, OUTPUT);

  if (!APDS.begin()) {
    Serial.println("Error initializing APDS9960 sensor!");
  }
}
```

In the loop() function, check if the proximity value is available using the APDS.proximityAvailable() function. Next, read sensor data by calling the APDS.readProximity() function.

```
void loop() {
  if (APDS.proximityAvailable()) {
    int proximity = APDS.readProximity();

    if(proximity<50){
      digitalWrite(LED_BUILTIN, HIGH);
    }else {
      digitalWrite(LED_BUILTIN, LOW);
    }

    // print value to the Serial Monitor
    Serial.println(proximity);
  }

  // wait a bit before reading again
  delay(100);
}
```

Save this program as ProximitySensor, then compile and upload it to the Arduino Nano 33 BLE Sense. You can try and put your hand next to the APDS9960 chip and then look at the proximity value in Serial Monitor. You can see the program output in Figure 3-20.

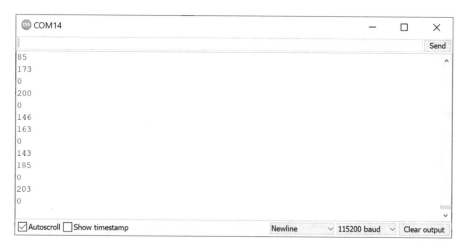

Figure 3-20. *Program output from ProximitySensor program*

Color Sensor

The APDS9960 chip has a color sensor. We will obtain an RGB value that consists of a red value, a green value, and a blue value. For this example, we read color from an object next to the APDS9960 chip.

Start by opening the Arduino software and creating a new program. Initialize serial communication and the APDS9960 chip by calling the APDS.begin() function.

```
#include <Arduino_APDS9960.h>

void setup() {
  Serial.begin(9600);
  while (!Serial);
```

```
  if (!APDS.begin()) {
    Serial.println("Error initializing APDS9960 sensor.");
  }
}
```

In the loop() function, check if the color sensor data are available using the APDS.colorAvailable() function. Then, we read the sensor using APDS.readColor(). You will obtain three values— Red, Green, and Blue—and print them to the serial terminal.

```
void loop() {
  // check if a color reading is available
  while (! APDS.colorAvailable()) {
    delay(5);
  }
  int r, g, b;

  // read the color
  APDS.readColor(r, g, b);

  // print the values
  Serial.print("r = ");
  Serial.println(r);
  Serial.print("g = ");
  Serial.println(g);
  Serial.print("b = ");
  Serial.println(b);
  Serial.println();

  // wait a bit before reading again
  delay(1000);
}
```

Save this program as ColorSensor, then compile and upload it to the Arduino Nano 33 BLE Sense. You can try to put any color next to the APDS9960 chip and then view the color sensor value in Serial Monitor. The program output in Figure 3-21 was obtained from a white object. You should probably use additional light if you are in a low-lit room.

Figure 3-21. *Program output from ColorSensor*

Gesture Sensor

The last sensor from the APDS9960 chip is a gesture sensor. We can perform four gestures on this chip, in the following directions.

- UP: From USB connector toward antenna.

- DOWN: From antenna toward USB connector.

- LEFT: From the analog pins side toward the digital pins side.

- RIGHT: From the digital pins side toward the analog pins side.

In this demo scenario, we develop Sketch program to turn on an LED when a user performs a gesture in the UP and RIGHT directions. Otherwise, the LED will be off.

Start by opening the Arduino software and creating a new program. Initialize serial communication and the APDS9960 chip by calling the APDS.begin() function.

```
#include <Arduino_APDS9960.h>

void setup() {
  Serial.begin(115200);
  while (!Serial);

  pinMode(LED_BUILTIN, OUTPUT);

  if (!APDS.begin()) {
    Serial.println("Error initializing APDS9960 sensor!");
  }

  Serial.println("Detecting gestures ...");
}
```

In the loop() function, check if the gesture sensor data are available using the APDS.gestureAvailable() function. Then, read the sensor using APDS.readGesture(). You will obtain four values: GESTURE_UP, GESTURE_DOWN, GESTURE_LEFT, and GESTURE_RIGHT. When you have sensor values for GESTURE_UP and GESTURE_RIGHT, the LED will turn on. Otherwise, the LED will be turned off.

```
void loop() {
  if (APDS.gestureAvailable()) {
    // a gesture was detected, read and print to serial monitor
    int gesture = APDS.readGesture();
```

```
switch (gesture) {
  case GESTURE_UP:
    Serial.println("Detected UP gesture");
    digitalWrite(LED_BUILTIN, HIGH);
    break;

  case GESTURE_DOWN:
    Serial.println("Detected DOWN gesture");
    digitalWrite(LED_BUILTIN, LOW);
    break;

  case GESTURE_LEFT:
    Serial.println("Detected LEFT gesture");
    digitalWrite(LED_BUILTIN, LOW);
    break;

  case GESTURE_RIGHT:
    Serial.println("Detected RIGHT gesture");
    digitalWrite(LED_BUILTIN, HIGH);
    break;

  default:
    // ignore
    break;
  }
 }
}
```

Save this program as GestureSensor, the compile and upload it to the Arduino Nano 33 BLE Sense. You can see the program output in Serial Monitor.

You can move your hand or object from the USB connector toward the antenna (UP direction) or from the digital pins side toward the analog pins side (RIGHT direction). As a result, you should see a lit LED on the Arduino Nano 33 BLE Sense. You also can perform a DOWN or LEFT direction gesture to turn off the LED. The example output in Figure 3-22 is the result of some gesture directions.

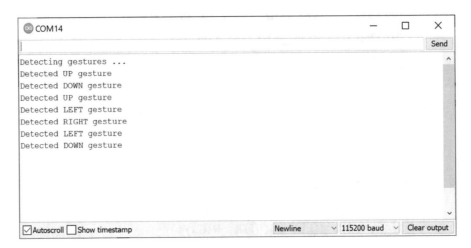

Figure 3-22. *Program output from the GestureSensor program*

You can continue to practice developing Sketch programs by applying the built-in sensors in the Arduino Nano 33 BLE Sense board.

Summary

This chapter covered how to access internal sensors in the Arduino Nano 33 BLE Sense board. We have built Sketch programs to access an IMU, a pressure sensor, a digital microphone, a humidity and temperature sensor, and a gesture sensor. We also plotted sensor data using the Serial Plotter tool and an OLED I2C display.

Next, we turn to working with BLE on the Arduino Nano 33 BLE Sense board.

CHAPTER 4

Bluetooth Low Energy

The Arduino Nano 33 BLE Sense board is built from the nRF52840 processor from Nordic. This processor has a Bluetooth and BLE radio module. In this chapter, we explore how to get started with BLE on the Arduino Nano 33 BLE Sense. We will build programs to use this BLE module.

You will learn about the following topics in this chapter:

- Setting up a BLE library on Arduino Nano 33 BLE Sense.

- Building a simple BLE application.

- Developing an LED control program over BLE.

- Exposing sensor data over the BLE service.

Introduction

The Arduino Nano 33 BLE Sense board is an IoT platform from Arduino. This board uses a Bluetooth module to connect to a network. Arduino Nano 33 BLE Sense includes support for BLE radio. BLE technology enables users to advertise services and allows interactions among BLE devices such as mobile devices.

© Agus Kurniawan 2021
A. Kurniawan, *IoT Projects with Arduino Nano 33 BLE Sense*,
https://doi.org/10.1007/978-1-4842-6458-4_4

Each BLE radio can act as a bulletin board or a reader. When it serves as a bulletin board, we can expose some data for all BLE radios, which are BLE readers. The BLE specification also provides a notification mechanism to alert readers when data are changed.

In this chapter, we explore how to work with BLE on the Arduino Nano 33 BLE Sense. Next, we set up a BLE library to work with BLE radio on the Arduino Nano 33 BLE Sense.

Setting up Bluetooth Low Energy

To work with BLE on the Arduino Nano 33 BLE Sense, you need the ArduinoBLE library. You can then perform BLE operations such as making and advertising BLE services. Details of the ArduinoBLE library can be found at `https://www.arduino.cc/en/Reference/ArduinoBLE`.

You can open Library Manager from the Sketch menu by selecting Include Library ➤ Manage Libraries. Once those options are selected, you will see the screen shown in Figure 4-1.

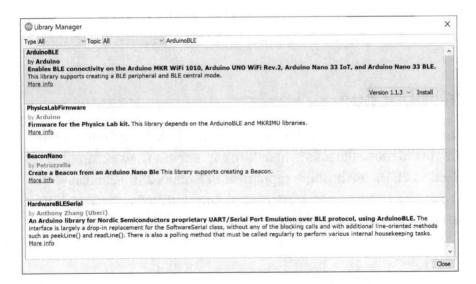

Figure 4-1. *Adding the ArduinoBLE library*

Type ArduinoBLE in the search text box and press Enter. You should see the ArduinoBLE library in the resulting form. Select this library and click Install. Once installation is complete, you can build an Arduino program to apply BLE radio.

Demo 1: Hello Arduino BLE

In the first demo we will build a Hello World application for BLE radio. We advertise our BLE with a specific BLE name. If the BLE reader is connected, we will set it to turn on the LED. When the BLE reader is disconnected, we will set it to turn off the LED. The next step is to write a program with the Arduino software.

Writing Sketch Program

We will develop Arduino program to advertise the BLE service and turn on the LED after the BLE reader is connected. Start by opening the Arduino software. Create a new program. Next, write codes step-by-step.

First, import the ArduinoBLE library into the program by adding this code.

```
#include <ArduinoBLE.h>
```

In the setup() function, initialize serial communication, the LED, and BLE radio. Call Serial.begin() to initialize serial communication with a baud rate value of 115200. Set the LED pin on LED_BUILTIN as OUTPUT mode. To activate BLE radio on the Arduino Nano 33 BLE Sense, we call the BLE.begin() function.

```
void setup() {
  Serial.begin(115200);
  while (!Serial);

  pinMode(LED_BUILTIN, OUTPUT);
```

```
// begin initialization
if (!BLE.begin()) {
  Serial.println("starting BLE failed!");
  while (1);
}
```

Next, set your BLE radio name by calling `BLE.setLocalName()`. This name will be detected on the BLE reader. Set the BLE UUID by calling the `BLE.setAdvertisedServiceUuid()` function. BLE UUID represents a computed 128-bit value. You can generate UUID using the online tool available at `https://www.guidgenerator.com/online-guid-generator.aspx`.

```
BLE.setLocalName("HelloBLE");
BLE.setAdvertisedServiceUuid("19B10000-E8F2-537E-4F6C-
D104768A1214");
```

```
// start advertising
BLE.advertise();
Serial.println("Bluetooth device active, waiting for
connections...");
}
```

Make sure your BLE UUID complies with standard BLE SIG. Some BLE UUIDs are reserved by their services. You can check these services at `https://www.bluetooth.com/specifications/assigned-numbers/service-discovery/`.

Next, we wait for the incoming BLE reader on the `loop()` function. We can call `BLE.contral()` to wait for BLE readers.

```
void loop() {
  // wait for a BLE central
  BLEDevice central = BLE.central();
```

After the BLE reader is connected to your BLE radio on the Arduino Nano 33 BLE Sense, we can obtain the BLEDevice object. Then, turn on LED by calling digitalWrite() with a passing HIGH value. Then, we perform infinite looping checking the connection status.

```
if (central) {
  Serial.print("Connected to central: ");
  Serial.println(central.address());
  digitalWrite(LED_BUILTIN, HIGH);

  while (central.connected()) {
    // do nothing
  }
```

If the BLE reader is disconnected, you will obtain a false value from central.connected(). After that, turn off the LED by calling digitalWrite() with a passing LOW value.

```
  digitalWrite(LED_BUILTIN, LOW);
  Serial.print("Disconnected from central: ");
  Serial.println(central.address());
  }
}
```

Your program is done. You can save this program as HelloBLE.

Testing Program

Now your Arduino program HelloBLE can be compiled and uploaded to the Arduino Nano 33 BLE Sense. To test the program, you will need a mobile phone with an Android or iOS platform. This demo uses an Android phone.

First, open Serial Monitor to view the program output from the HelloBLE program. Next, download the nRF Connect for Mobile application from the Google Play Store, as shown in Figure 4-2, or Apple Store.

Figure 4-2. *nRF Connect for Mobile application in the Google Play Store*

Download and install the nRF Connect for Mobile application for your mobile platform. After it is installed, you can run this program. You can see the initial result of running this application on Android in Figure 4-3. The next step is to connect to the Arduino Nano 33 BLE Sense.

Figure 4-3. *A form of nRF Connect for Mobile application*

Tap SCAN on the device to obtain a list of BLE devices. You should see the HelloBLE service, as highlighted in Figure 4-4. If you don't see it, try tapping SCAN again.

Figure 4-4. *HelloBLE service is displayed*

Next tap CONNECT for HelloBLE, highlighted in Figure 4-4. After that, you are connected the to Arduino Nano 33 BLE Sense board over BLE radio. Figure 4-5 shows that this Android phone is connected to the HelloBLE service from the Arduino Nano 33 BLE Sense.

Figure 4-5. *Connected to HelloBLE service*

To disconnect from the HelloBLE service, you can tap DISCONNECT. That causes the mobile device to close BLE radio communication. If you already opened Serial Monitor, you will see all event messages on this tool. You can view program output in Serial Monitor in Figure 4-6.

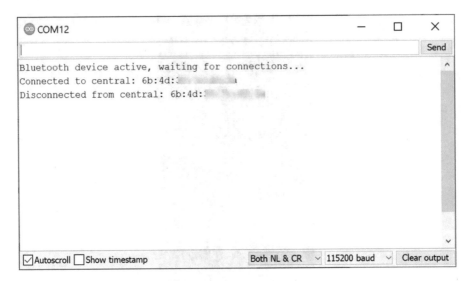

Figure 4-6. *Program output in Serial Monitor from HelloBLE*

Demo 2: Controlling an LED with BLE

In this demo, we will build an LED controller over BLE radio using the BLE service to expose the LED service. We can turn the LED on and off LED using a mobile application. For implementation, we use a program sample from Arduino, LED. Next, we develop Sketch program.

Writing Program

We will develop an Arduino program to control an LED over BLE radio. Start by opening the Arduino software to create a new program. Next, we write the code step-by-step.

First, import the ArduinoBLE library into your program and initialize the BLE Service with BLERead and BLEWrite characteristics. Define ledPin for LED_BUILTIN. Write the following code.

```
#include <ArduinoBLE.h>
```

```
BLEService ledService("19B10000-E8F2-537E-4F6C-D104768A1214");
BLEByteCharacteristic switchCharacteristic("19B10001-E8F2-537E-
4F6C-D104768A1214", BLERead | BLEWrite);

const int ledPin = LED_BUILTIN;
```

Next, initialize serial communication and digital OUTPUT mode on the setup() function. In addition, initialize BLE radio on the Arduino Nano 33 BLE Sense using the BLE.begin() function.

```
void setup() {
  Serial.begin(9600);
  while (!Serial);

  // set LED pin to output mode
  pinMode(ledPin, OUTPUT);

  // begin initialization
  if (!BLE.begin()) {
    Serial.println("starting BLE failed!");

    while (1);
  }
```

Next, set the BLE service and characteristics using the addCharacteristic() function, and then initialize characteristic values by calling the writeValue() function.

```
  // set advertised local name and service UUID:
  BLE.setLocalName("LED");
  BLE.setAdvertisedService(ledService);

  // add the characteristic to the service
  ledService.addCharacteristic(switchCharacteristic);

  // add service
```

```
BLE.addService(ledService);

// set the initial value for the characteristic:
switchCharacteristic.writeValue(0);
```

After you have defined your BLE service, you can start to advertise using the BLE.advertise() function. Print a message for information that our BLE is ready for incoming BLE readers.

```
// start advertising
BLE.advertise();

Serial.println("BLE LED Peripheral");
}
```

In the loop() function, we wait for BLE readers. Use BLE.central(). If the BLE reader is connected to the Arduino Nano 33 BLE Sense, you will obtain a BLEDevice object.

```
void loop() {
  BLEDevice central = BLE.central();
```

After the BLE reader is connected to the Arduino Nano 33 BLE Sense, print the media access control (MAC) address from the BLE reader. Next, we perform a loop and wait for input data from the BLE reader using the value() function

....
....
....
....000000-
00000000000000000000000000000000000000000000 from the BLE service characteristic. If the user sends data with a value greater than 0, the LED will be turned on; otherwise, it will be turned off.

```
if (central) {
  Serial.print("Connected to central: ");
  // print the central's MAC address:
  Serial.println(central.address());

  // while the central is still connected to peripheral:
  while (central.connected()) {
    // if the remote device wrote to the characteristic,
    // use the value to control the LED:
    if (switchCharacteristic.written()) {
      int val = switchCharacteristic.value();
      Serial.println(val);
      if (val>0) {    // any value other than 0
        Serial.println("LED on");
        digitalWrite(ledPin, HIGH);        // will turn the
                                           LED on
      } else {                             // a 0 value
        Serial.println(F("LED off"));
        digitalWrite(ledPin, LOW);         // will turn the
                                           LED off
      }
    }
  }
}
```

Finally, print the message to the serial terminal if the BLE reader disconnects.

```
  Serial.print(F("Disconnected from central: "));
  Serial.println(central.address());
  }
}
```

Our program is done. You can save this program as LED.

Testing Program

Now your Arduino program, LED, can be compiled and uploaded to the Arduino Nano 33 BLE Sense. To test this program, you need a mobile phone using the Android or iOS platform. This demo uses an Android phone.

First, open Serial Monitor to see the output from the LED program. Now you can open the nRF Connect for Mobile application from your platform. You should see the BLE service on this application, as shown in Figure 4-7. Tap CONNECT to connect to the Arduino Nano 33 BLE Sense.

Figure 4-7. *LED service shows in nRF Connect for Mobile application*

After it is connected, you will see the form shown in Figure 4-8. You can expand the BLE service characteristics. There are two properties: READ and WRITE.

Figure 4-8. *Display showing the BLE service characteristics*

Tap WRITE. Next, set a value of 15 to turn on the LED, as illustrated in Figure 4-9. Tap SEND to send this value. You should see the LED light up on the Arduino Nano 33 BLE Sense. You also can send a value of 00 to turn off the LED on the WRITE property, as shown in Figure 4-10.

Figure 4-9. *Writing a value of 15 to turn on the LED*

Figure 4-10. *Writing a value of 00 to turn off the LED*

If you have already opened Serial Monitor, you will see the program's output events information, as shown in Figure 4-11.

127

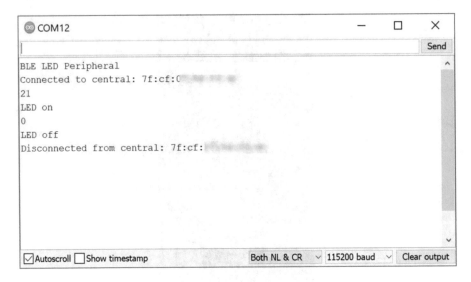

Figure 4-11. *Program output from LED*

Demo 3: Sensor Real-Time Monitoring

In this section, we will build a sensor real-time monitoring system over BLE radio. We will create a BLE service that provides temperature and humidity sensor data to the BLE reader. You can modify your previous project, TempHumidity. The BLE reader will be notified if the sensor data changes.

We will expose sensor data from the HTS221 chip over the BLE service so the BLE reader can read this sensor data after it is connected to the Arduino Nano 33 BLE Sense.

The next step is to build a Sketch program to implement the demo. This example uses an Android mobile phone.

Writing Program

We need to create a new Arduino program to create a BLE service and then broadcast the temperature and humidity sensor data to BLE readers. We will create a BLE service with three characteristics, each of which will expose temperature and humidity sensors.

To get started, open the Arduino software. First, call the required libraries.

```
#include <ArduinoBLE.h>
#include <Arduino_HTS221.h>
```

Next, define the BLE service and three BLE characteristics. You need a different UUID to apply these features. You must also define three variables to hold sensor data.

```
BLEService sensorService("16150f38-e7a9-4fe1-ae08-
48464baf25b2");
BLEStringCharacteristic  temperatureSensorLevel("ff99948c-18ff-
4ed8-942e-512b9b24b6da",
    BLERead | BLENotify,15);
BLEStringCharacteristic  humiditySensorLevel("8084aa6b-6cae-
461f-9540-e1a5768de49d",
    BLERead | BLENotify,15);

// last sensor data
float oldTemperature = 0;
float oldHumidity = 0;
```

In the setup() function, initialize serial communication with a baud rate value of 115200, HTS chip sensor, LED digital pin, and BLE module.

```
void setup() {
  Serial.begin(115200);
  while (!Serial);
```

```
if (!HTS.begin()) {
  Serial.println("Failed to initialize humidity temperature
  sensor!");
  while (1);
}

pinMode(LED_BUILTIN, OUTPUT);

if (!BLE.begin()) {
  Serial.println("starting BLE failed!");
  while (1);
}
```

Next, define the BLE service name and add it to the advertised service. Then, add all BLE characteristics into the BLE service.

```
BLE.setLocalName("TempHumidity");
BLE.setAdvertisedService(sensorService);

sensorService.addCharacteristic(temperatureSensorLevel);
  sensorService.addCharacteristic(humiditySensorLevel);
  BLE.addService(sensorService);
```

Set the initial default data on all BLE characteristics using the writeValue() function.

```
    temperatureSensorLevel.writeValue( String(oldTemperature));
  humiditySensorLevel.writeValue(String(oldHumidity));
```

Now we can start to advertise the BLE service by calling the BLE. advertise() function. BLE readers will recognize this BLE server.

```
BLE.advertise();
Serial.println("Bluetooth device active, waiting for
connections...");
}
```

In the loop() function, we await the incoming BLE reader. Once the BLE reader is connected, print the MAC address of BLE reader. Then, turn on the LED.

```
void loop() {
  BLEDevice central = BLE.central();
  if (central) {
    Serial.print("Connected to central: ");
    Serial.println(central.address());
    digitalWrite(LED_BUILTIN, HIGH);
```

If the BLE reader is connected, there will be a BLEDevice object. Perform a loop until the BLE reader is disconnected. Inside the loop, call the updateTempHumidityLevel() function to update sensor data to the BLE service.

```
    while (central.connected()) {
      //long currentMillis = millis();
      updateTempHumidityLevel ();
      delay(300);
    }
```

Turn off the LED after the BLE reader is disconnected.

```
    digitalWrite(LED_BUILTIN, LOW);
    Serial.print("Disconnected from central: ");
    Serial.println(central.address());
  }
}
```

For implementation of the updateTempHumidityLevel() function, read the temperature sensor using HTS.readTemperature(). Read the humidity sensor data using the HTS.readHumidity() function.

```
void updateTempHumidityLevel() {
```

```
float temp, hum;

temp = HTS.readTemperature();
hum = HTS.readHumidity();
```

Send temperature and humidity sensor data to the BLE service using the writeValue() function, and perform this task for all BLE characteristics.

```
if (temp != oldTemperature) {
    temperatureSensorLevel.writeValue(String(temp));
    oldTemperature = temp;
}
if (hum != oldHumidity) {
    humiditySensorLevel.writeValue(String(hum));
    oldHumidity = hum;
}

Serial.print(temp);
Serial.print('\t');
Serial.println(hum);
```
}

Save this program as TempHumidityBLEService.

Testing

Compile and upload the TempHumidityBLEService program into the Arduino Nano 33 BLE Sense board. Next, use the nRF Connect for Mobile application. Tap SCAN to display a list of BLE services in your environment.

Figure 4-12 shows the TempHumidity BLE service detected on the nRF Connect for Mobile application. Tap CONNECT to connect the TempHumidity BLE service.

Figure 4-12. *Detecting the TempHumidity BLE service*

After this is connected, you will see the properties and characteristics of the TempHumidity BLE service as shown in Figure 4-13.

Figure 4-13. *Connected to the TempHumidity BLE service*

You can expand Unknown Service to see the BLE characteristics. After it is expanded, you will see three BLE characteristics that represent TempHumidity sensor data, displayed in Figure 4-14.

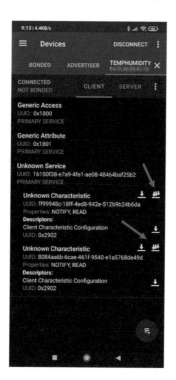

Figure 4-14. *Opening BLE characteristics from the TempHumidity BLE service*

Tap the arrow array icon highlighted in Figure 4-14. That will show you the sensor data from the temperature and humidity sensor. Figure 4-15 shows these temperature and humidity sensor data from the Arduino Nano 33 BLE Sense. The sensor data are signified by circles in Figure 4-15.

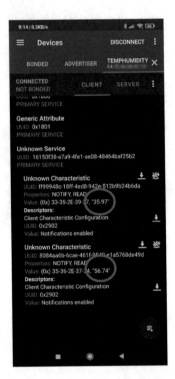

Figure 4-15. *Showing temperature and humidity sensors over the TempHumidity BLE service*

You can continue to practice by creating various BLE services. You also can build your own mobile application to consume BLE services.

Summary

This chapter explored how to set up a BLE radio on the Arduino Nano 33 BLE Sense board. You also built Arduino programs by applying BLE radio, starting by developing a hello world application. You also controlled an LED over BLE radio. Finally, you exposed temperature and humidity sensors to the BLE reader.

The next chapter covers how to implement embedded artificial intelligence on the Arduino Nano 33 BLE Sense.

CHAPTER 5

Embedded Artificial Intelligence

The Arduino Nano 33 BLE Sense with nRF8240 MCU enables us to perform artificial intelligence (AI) applications. You can use the TensorFlow Lite library to implement edge computing. This chapter explores how to get started with TensorFlow Lite on the Arduino Nano 33 BLE Sense.

You will learn about the following topics in this chapter:

- Setting up the TensorFlow Lite library.

- Developing embedded AI applications.

- Building a gesture classification.

Introduction

The Arduino Nano 33 BLE Sense has support for embedded AI using TensorFlow. In this chapter, we explore how to get started with the TensorFlow Lite library on the Arduino Nano 33 BLE Sense. All demos are run on a Windows 10 machine.

© Agus Kurniawan 2021
A. Kurniawan, *IoT Projects with Arduino Nano 33 BLE Sense*,
https://doi.org/10.1007/978-1-4842-6458-4_5

Setting Up TensorFlow Lite

To work with TensorFlow Lite, you should install it using Library Manager. Type arduino_tensorflowlite in the search text box. You should find this library as shown in Figure 5-1. Click Install to install the TensorFlow Lite library.

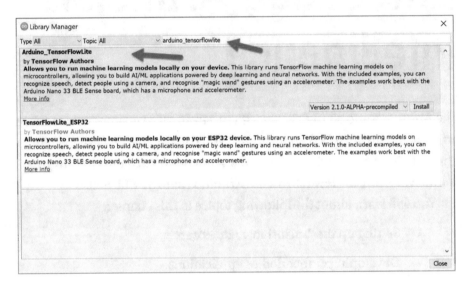

Figure 5-1. *Installing the TensorFlow Lite library*

Next, you can build TensorFlow Lite applications on the Arduino Nano 33 BLE Sense board.

Demo: Embedded Artificial Intelligence

TensorFlow is a machine learning framework. This library uses a deep learning algorithm for implementation. Deep learning is a form of supervised learning extended from neural networks. Machine learning and deep learning are outside the scope of this book, but you can research them if you are interested.

TensorFlow Lite is a light version of the TensorFlow framework. TensorFlow Lite is designed for small libraries and optimized for embedded boards. For a simple demonstration, we use a program sample. You can find program samples from the File menu by selecting Examples ➤ arduino_tensorflowlite. You should see hello_world. Click this program sample to obtain the program code shown in Figure 5-2.

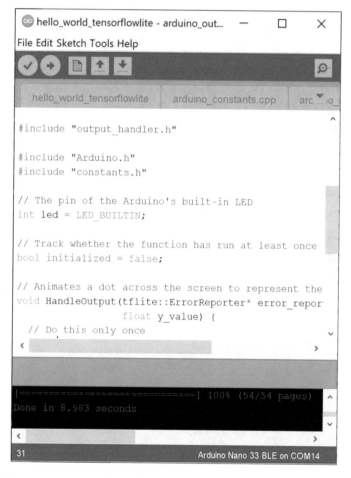

Figure 5-2. *A program from hello world and TensorFlow Lite*

Save this program as hello_world_tensorflowlite. After you save the program, you can check the program folder. You should see some files inside the program folder. Figure 5-3 shows some files from TensorFlow Lite program. This program performs prediction for sinusoid forms.

Name	Date modified	Type	Size
arduino_constants.cpp	9/20/2020 5:05 PM	C++ Source	1 KB
arduino_main.cpp	9/20/2020 5:05 PM	C++ Source	1 KB
arduino_output_handler.cpp	9/20/2020 5:05 PM	C++ Source	2 KB
constants.h	9/20/2020 5:05 PM	C/C++ Header	2 KB
hello_world_tensorflowlite.ino	9/20/2020 5:05 PM	Arduino file	5 KB
main_functions.h	9/20/2020 5:05 PM	C/C++ Header	2 KB
model.cpp	9/20/2020 5:05 PM	C++ Source	17 KB
model.h	9/20/2020 5:05 PM	C/C++ Header	2 KB
output_handler.h	9/20/2020 5:05 PM	C/C++ Header	2 KB

Figure 5-3. *A list of files in the hello world TensorFlow Lite program*

Now you can compile and upload this program into the Arduino Nano 33 BLE Sense. The compiling process might take a few minutes because this program will perform a training and then upload the program into the Arduino Nano 33 BLE Sense.

After uploading the program, you can open Serial Plotter, where you should see a graph of sinusoids. Figure 5-4 shows the program output from hello_world_tensorflowlite.

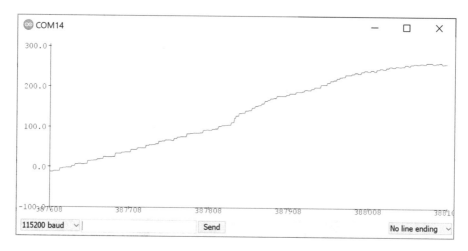

Figure 5-4. *Program output with Serial Plotter from hello world TensorFlow Lite program*

Gesture Classification

In this section, we will build an AI program from scratch using TensorFlow Lite on the Arduino Nano 33 BLE Sense. This project is modified from `https://github.com/arduino/ArduinoTensorFlowLiteTutorials`. Our scenario is to detect a gesture. For this demo, we want to detect a circle and line gesture movement as shown in Figure 5-5.

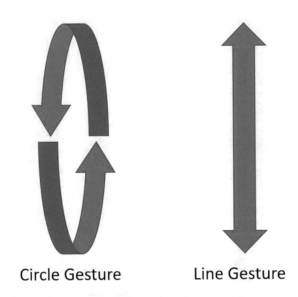

Circle Gesture   **Line Gesture**

Ground

Figure 5-5. *Gesture model forms for circle and line*

Circle and line gestures are movement forms in vertical mode as shown in Figure 5-5. This dataset is generated using the Arduino Nano BLE Sense with IMU sensor. For the training process, we use Python to perform machine learning computation with TensorFlow. You should install Python and some required libraries on your computer to perform the training dataset with TensorFlow.

To implement this project, you need to perform the following steps.

- Gathering a dataset.

- Building the model.

- Developing a classifier.

- Testing.

Gathering a Dataset

We use the Arduino Nano 33 BLE Sense to generate a dataset. Use the IMU sensor to capture acceleration and gyroscope from your gesture. In this project, we use a sample set of about 119 data values.

Open the Arduino software and create a new application. First, include the Arduino_LSM9DS1 library. Define the sample data size as 119 and define an acceleration threshold around 2.5.

```
#include <Arduino_LSM9DS1.h>

const float accelerationThreshold = 2.5; // threshold
const int numSamples = 119;

int samplesRead = numSamples;
```

In the setup() function, initialize serial communication and the IMU sensor by calling the IMU.begin() function. Print a data header on the serial terminal.

```
void setup() {
  Serial.begin(9600);
  while (!Serial);

  if (!IMU.begin()) {
    Serial.println("Failed to initialize IMU!");
    while (1);
  }
  // print the header
  Serial.println("aX,aY,aZ,gX,gY,gZ");
}
```

In the loop() function, check the data length for samplesRead and numSamples. If they have the same size, we calculate the sum of the sensor data from acceleration including setting the absolute value. Read acceleration sensor data using the IMU.readAcceleration() function.

```
void loop() {
  float aX, aY, aZ, gX, gY, gZ;

  // wait for significant motion
  while (samplesRead == numSamples) {
    if (IMU.accelerationAvailable()) {
      // read the acceleration data
      IMU.readAcceleration(aX, aY, aZ);

      // sum up the absolutes
      float aSum = fabs(aX) + fabs(aY) + fabs(aZ);

      // check if it's above the threshold
      if (aSum >= accelerationThreshold) {
        // reset the sample read count
        samplesRead = 0;
        break;
      }
    }
  }
}
```

If samplesRead size is below 119, proceed to read the data from the IMU sensor. Then, print them to the serial terminal.

```
  while (samplesRead < numSamples) {
    // check if both new acceleration and gyroscope data are
    // available
    if (IMU.accelerationAvailable() && IMU.
    gyroscopeAvailable()) {
      // read the acceleration and gyroscope data
```

```
IMU.readAcceleration(aX, aY, aZ);
IMU.readGyroscope(gX, gY, gZ);

samplesRead++;

// print the data in CSV format
Serial.print(aX, 3);
Serial.print(',');
Serial.print(aY, 3);
Serial.print(',');
Serial.print(aZ, 3);
Serial.print(',');
Serial.print(gX, 3);
Serial.print(',');
Serial.print(gY, 3);
Serial.print(',');
Serial.print(gZ, 3);
Serial.println();

if (samplesRead == numSamples) {
  // add an empty line if it's the last sample
  Serial.println();
}
    }
  }
}
```

Save this program as IMU_GetData, then compile and upload it into the Arduino Nano 33 BLE Sense. To test our program to generate a dataset, perform the following tasks.

- Press the Reset button on the Arduino Nano 33 BLE Sense board.

- Open Serial Monitor.

- Hold the board with your hand.

- Make a movement like the vertical circle shown in Figure 5-5.

- Generate these data for at least 10 samples.

- Each sample data (119 data points) is separated by Carriage Return, Line Feed (CRLF).

Figure 5-6 shows a result of the generated data set after the vertical circle gesture is performed. Copy and paste these data to a text editor such as Notepad in Windows.

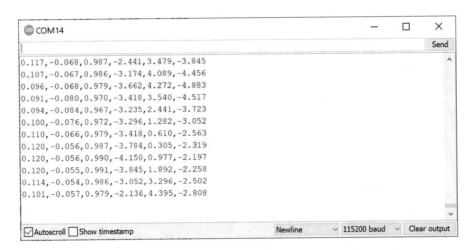

Figure 5-6. *Sensor data after the circle gesture is performed*

For the dataset in Figure 5-7, 31 data samples have been generated. Save these data as circle.csv. Perform a similar task for the vertical line gesture (see Figure 5-5). Copy and paste the result of generating the line gesture to a text editor. Save the file as line.csv.

You now have two datasets, circle.csv and line.csv. You will use those files for training in deep learning computation using TensorFlow.

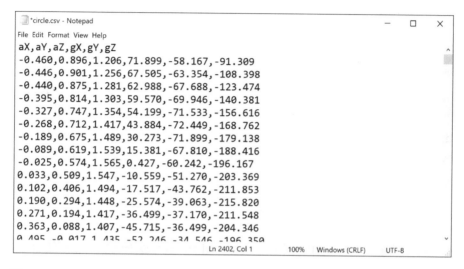

Figure 5-7. *Storing sensor dataset to a CSV file*

Building the Model

In this section, we build a model in a computer. Performing a heavy machine learning task on an embedded board is difficult because hardware resources are limited. We therefore implement deep learning computation on a computer.

First, your computer should have Python installed. This demo uses Python version 3.8.x. You can download and install Python for your platform from https://www.python.org/downloads/. For Windows, make sure you checked that it is installed on PATH so the Windows command prompt can recognize the Python commands. For Linux, you should install Python pip with own platform. For instance, you can install pip in Ubuntu using this command.

```
$ sudo apt install python3-pip
```

After Python is installed, you can open terminal or Windows command prompts and type this command.

```
$ python --version
$ pip --version
```

You should see Python and the pip version on your terminal.

Next, install Python libraries such as Pandas and Numpy. You should also install Jupyter Notebook for the Python editor. To learn more about Jupyter Notebook, visit the official website at `https://jupyter.org/`. You can install all required libraries using the `pip` command. Type these commands.

```
$ pip install pandas numpy matplotlib
$ pip install notebook
```

You also should install TensorFlow for Python on your computer. To do so, you can type this command.

```
$ pip install tensorflow
```

This installation process takes a few minutes to complete. If you have errors regarding a C++ compiler, you should install GCC on Linux/macOS or Visual C++ on Windows.

Now you can navigate to any working folder where the circle.csv and line.csv files are located. Then, run your Jupyter Notebook by typing this command.

```
$ jupyter notebook
```

You should then see a browser open. You can then create a new application and create a Python program inside this notebook. A complete program can be found in the source codes for this book. Find the file Gesture Training.ipynb. Put this file inside your working folder. After opening it, you should have a form like the one shown in Figure 5-8.

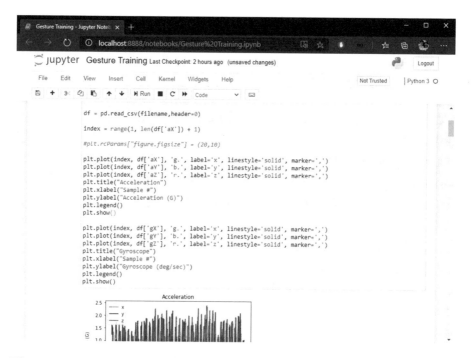

Figure 5-8. *Jupyter Notebook runs a Python program*

Now, let's explain this program. First, load all required libraries on Python.

```
import matplotlib
%matplotlib inline
```

```
import matplotlib.pyplot as plt
import numpy as np
import pandas as pd
```

```
import tensorflow as tf
print(f"TensorFlow version = {tf.__version__}\n")
```

Next, plot the dataset. For instance, open the circle.csv file And use the Matplotlib library to visualize the data. You should read the Matplotlib documentation at `https://matplotlib.org/3.3.1/contents.html`.

```python
filename = "circle.csv"
df = pd.read_csv(filename,header=0)
index = range(1, len(df['aX']) + 1)
#plt.rcParams["figure.figsize"] = (20,10)

plt.plot(index, df['aX'], 'g.', label='x', linestyle='solid',
marker=',')
plt.plot(index, df['aY'], 'b.', label='y', linestyle='solid',
marker=',')
plt.plot(index, df['aZ'], 'r.', label='z', linestyle='solid',
marker=',')
plt.title("Acceleration")
plt.xlabel("Sample #")
plt.ylabel("Acceleration (G)")
plt.legend()
plt.show()

plt.plot(index, df['gX'], 'g.', label='x', linestyle='solid',
marker=',')
plt.plot(index, df['gY'], 'b.', label='y', linestyle='solid',
marker=',')
plt.plot(index, df['gZ'], 'r.', label='z', linestyle='solid',
marker=',')
plt.title("Gyroscope")
plt.xlabel("Sample #")
plt.ylabel("Gyroscope (deg/sec)")
plt.legend()
plt.show()
```

After running these scripts on Jupyter Notebook, you should see a graph of the circle.csv file as shown in Figure 5-9. If you change the filename value to line.csv, you will see a graph of line.csv, as shown in Figure 5-10.

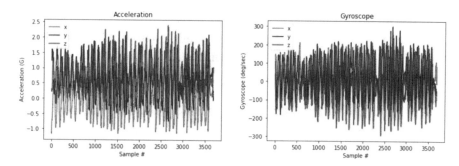

Figure 5-9. *Plotting dataset for the circle gesture*

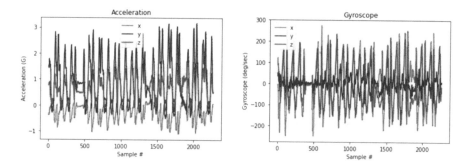

Figure 5-10. *Plotting dataset for the line gesture*

After that, read all of the data from the circle.csv and line.csv files. Then split the dataset for training and testing. To build a model, use TensorFlow and Keras (https://keras.io/). You can see the following Tensor architecture for your project.

```
# build the model and train it
model = tf.keras.Sequential()
model.add(tf.keras.layers.Dense(50, activation='relu')) # relu
is used for performance
model.add(tf.keras.layers.Dense(15, activation='relu'))
model.add(tf.keras.layers.Dense(NUM_GESTURES,
activation='softmax')) # softmax is used, because we only
expect one gesture to occur per input
```

```
model.compile(optimizer='rmsprop', loss='mse', metrics=['mae'])
history = model.fit(inputs_train, outputs_train, epochs=600,
batch_size=1, validation_data=(inputs_validate, outputs_
validate))
```

These scripts take a few minutes to complete the training phase. Set the epochs value to 600.

Next, you need to save your model into a file. Store the model in a TensorFlow Lite form.

```
converter = tf.lite.TFLiteConverter.from_keras_model(model)
tflite_model = converter.convert()

# Save the model to disk
open("gesture_model.tflite", "wb").write(tflite_model)

import os
basic_model_size = os.path.getsize("gesture_model.tflite")
print("Model is %d bytes" % basic_model_size)
```

These scripts generate a model file called gesture_model.tflite. You can check it in the working folder. Next, convert the content of gesture_model. tflite to a model.h file. Technically, you will convert a binary file to a hex string. For Linux/macOS, you can run these scripts.

```
# linux / mac
!echo "const unsigned char model[] = {" > model.h
!cat gesture_model.tflite | xxd -i       >> model.h
!echo "};"                               >> model.h

import os
model_h_size = os.path.getsize("model.h")
print(f"Header file, model.h, is {model_h_size:,} bytes.")
print("\nOpen the side panel (refresh if needed). Double click
model.h to download the file.")
```

If you have a problem for xxd, you should install it. For Debian/ Ubuntu, you can install it using these commands.

```
$ sudo apt update
$ sudo apt install xxd
```

Because Windows does not have an xxd application, we can use xxd from the Vim application. Download and install Vim for Windows from https://www.vim.org/download.php. After it is installed, you can copy xxd.exe to a working folder. You should also change the cat command to a type command in Windows. You can run these scripts.

```
# windows
!echo const unsigned char model[] = { > model.h
!type gesture_model.tflite | xxd.exe -i      >> model.h
!echo };                                 >> model.h

import os
model_h_size = os.path.getsize("model.h")
print(f"Header file, model.h, is {model_h_size:,} bytes.")
print("\nOpen the side panel (refresh if needed). Double click
model.h to download the file.")
```

Now you have a model.h file, which you can use for an Arduino Sketch program. Figure 5-11 shows the content of the model.h file.

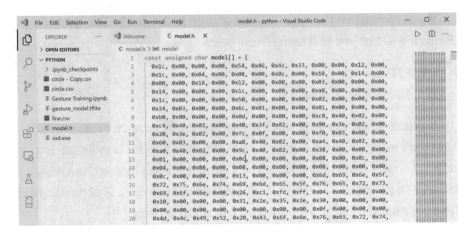

Figure 5-11.   *Content of model.h file*

Developing a Classifier

In this section, we will build an Arduino Sketch program to detect a circle and line gestures. You can create a new program using Arduino. Save this program as IMU_Classifier. Next, put model.h from our model into this program folder.

For this demonstration, we modify the IMU_Classifier codes program at https://github.com/arduino/ArduinoTensorFlowLiteTutorials. Set the gesture models for circle and line.

```
...
// array to map gesture index to a name
const char* GESTURES[] = {
  "circle",
  "line"
};
...
```

Save this program. Make sure that your model, the model.h file, is already in this program folder. Compile and upload the program to the Arduino Nano 33 BLE Sense. It takes a few minutes to complete this task.

Testing

After you have uploaded the program, you can test it. Open Serial Monitor, then make a vertical circle gesture. You can see in Figure 5-12 that the confidence value for the circle is higher than the confidence level for a line gesture.

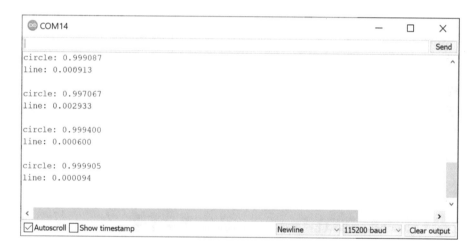

Figure 5-12. *Program output after performing a circle gesture*

Next, you can try to make a vertical line gesture. You can then see from Figure 5-13 that the confidence level for a line is higher than the confidence level for a circle gesture.

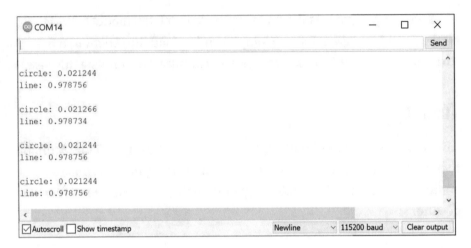

Figure 5-13. *Program output after performing a line gesture*

If you make random gestures, check to see what the confidence level values for circles and lines are. You can continue your practice by developing some AI programs with TensorFlow Lite and the Arduino Nano 33 BLE Sense.

Summary

This chapter addressed how to explore TensorFlow Lite on the Arduino Nano 33 BLE Sense. We ran a program sample for hello world, and then we created our own gesture classification with the TensorFlow Lite library on the Arduino Nano 33 BLE Sense and with Python TensorFlow on a computer.

Index

© Agus Kurniawan 2021
A. Kurniawan, *IoT Projects with Arduino Nano 33 BLE Sense*,
https://doi.org/10.1007/978-1-4842-6458-4

Printed in the United States
By Bookmasters